A FLOWER
BLOOMING
IN THE DARK

Memoirs and poems of Chicago from the youth who shape it

A FLOWER BLOOMING IN THE DARK

Cover and Interior Illustrations: Joe Mills // joemills.com
Director of Programs: Maria Villarreal
Publications Coordinator: Waringa Hunja
Managing Editors: Shannon Barry and Kate Kowalski
Copy Editors: Shannon Barry, Kate Kowalski, Breanne Johnson, Mary Norkol

Proceeds from your purchase of this publication support 826CHI, a non-profit creative writing, tutoring, and publishing center. www.826chi.org

Printed in the United States by McNaughton & Gunn

TABLE of CONTENTS

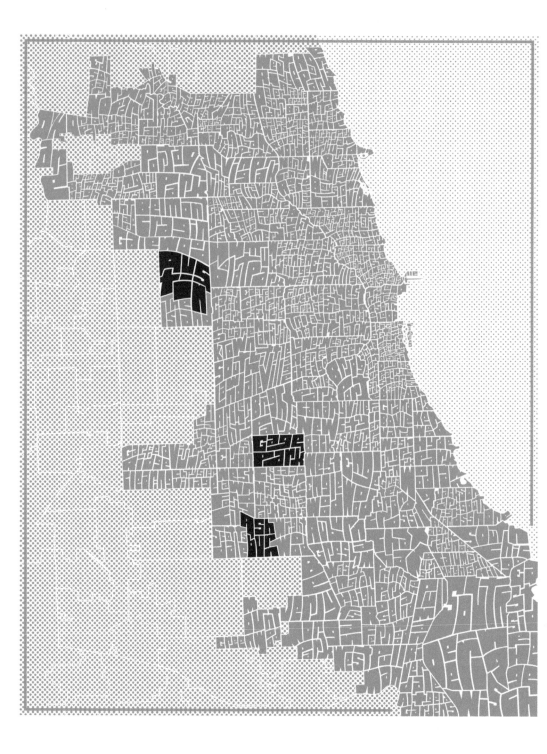

FOREWORD

BY DR. EVE L. EWING

"There is always something new to love and admire about this city," writes fourteen-year-old Anai C. in her prose piece about the annual Ferris wheel ride she takes with her family. I understand what she means. Reading her work reminded me of the last time I rode that same Ferris wheel, at Navy Pier, with my niece, who is five. She pressed her face against the glass in a mix of giddiness and fear, and I watched her with the same knotted stomach that Anai describes.

There is always something new to love. Reading this collection of poems and prose pieces from young people all across our beloved Chicago, this much is clear. The writers come from all corners of the city. Each comes to the page with a different story; they are different ages, races, genders, and have different interests. In fact, I have to admit that reading the bios of each writer is almost as fun as reading their actual work—like this one:

Luis C. (eighth grade) is an eighth grader (duh) in Chicago whose hobbies include playing guitar, playing sports, reading, building things, watching Youtube, playing video games, and being overly sarcastic (notice how he didn't say writing). He is a giant nerd on many things including being weird, comics, Rick and Morty, video games, books, math, science, Greek and Roman mythology, believing conspiracy theories, books, and social studies (notice how he still didn't say writing).

For someone who allegedly doesn't like writing, Luis, that was... well, that was some writing.

But what all of these young authors share is an incisive view of the city we call home, one that transcends any effort at flat rendering from outside folks who simply don't know what they're talking about because they're not from here. (Poor them.) Their telling is careful and honest, and these writers made me laugh (Daniel D., you got me with "The city of the Chicago hot dog / Soft poppy seed bun with a tangy bam that hits harder than your Auntie Pam"). They broke my heart, as when Angel J. G. wrote, "When he calls to check on his mother, brothers, and sisters, she either answers or she doesn't, but at least he tries." They made me gasp with recognition, as when thirteen-year-old Luz Q. wrote of a childhood summer night spent making mischief with her neighborhood crew. "We were complete champions, even if our knees were scraped, even if our hair looked like lions, even if our mouths were full of thirst, every 'if' didn't matter, we were completely free."

They also reminded me that there is beauty everywhere, if you know how to look. Consider the anonymous writer who describes a night out with their fellow graffiti artists, searching for the perfect place to paint. "The lights shined a golden filter down the all-too-familiar Chicago alley: gang graffiti on the garages, broken glass on the rugged pavement, and a few dumpster rats, of course." When they hop on the train the next morning among the indifferent commuters, they beam with pride at their secret achievement. "All along the rooftops were pieces of graffiti. It was like the South Side's own ghetto art gallery. Most people on the train couldn't care less about the pieces of vandalism that surrounded them. When our pieces came up, we gazed with pride, knowing that that was our own exhibit." This writer has given us a great gift, reminding us to pause and look out the window every once in a while rather than miss the secret masterpieces the city has in store for us.

"Chicago is a flower blooming in the dark," writes Monsse R. I gasped when I read that—not only because it's such a lovely turn of phrase, but because it also seems like an apt description of the writers themselves. They are blooming before our very eyes, and how lucky we are to witness their light.

Dr. Eve L. Ewing is a sociologist of education and a writer from Chicago. She is the author of *Electric Arches*, which received awards from the American Library Association and the Poetry Society of America and was named one of the year's best books by NPR and the Chicago Tribune. She is also author of *Ghosts in the Schoolyard: Racism and School Closings on Chicago's South Side* and the co-author (with Nate Marshall) of *No Blue Memories: The Life of Gwendolyn Brooks*. She is a scholar at the University of Chicago School of Social Service Administration. Her work has been published in The New Yorker, The Atlantic, The New York Times, and many other venues.

STUDENT FOREWORD

by the student ambassadors at Pathways in Education: Jaylin, Paola, Jamia, Izzy, Jonathan, Hannah, and Riley

If you can survive here you can survive anywhere.

In this book we share our stories, our lessons, our views, our feelings, and our city with you. This book is filled with writing from teens all over the city. You might read pieces that are set in the same part of the city or that deal with the same sort of topic, but we want you to know that our perspectives are unique. Our hope is to give you, the reader, a better view of Chicago. We're fully aware of all the stereotypes that plague our city. It's OK to have your own perception of Chicago, but don't be surprised by what you read here because we wrote about our specific connection to this city. We heard each other talk about relationships, the EL, Navy Pier, block parties, graffitti, addiction, ChinaTown, ice skating, and so much more. This brought us closer together.

We want you to understand that through the writing process we reflected on our lives in Chicago. It wasn't easy to write out our feelings and thoughts. It definitely wasn't an easy choice for some of us to share about our hardships, but we knew that we would be contributing to creating a more complete story of our city. A story that is often not put on display for the city at large or the nation to hear and know.

It's OK to skip around in this book or read it straight through. We hope that by reading this book (in any way you choose) you begin to see that there's more to Chicago. We hope to ignite in you a curiosity to explore, research, and learn more about the city, northside to southside, lakeside to westside.

No matter what you've heard about Chicago we want you to dig deeper. We want you to know us, to hear our voices, and understand that our city has cultures and subcultures. That we and Chicago are layered, complex, and complicated. We and Chicago are soft, welcoming, and empathetic. We and Chicago are more than what you see in your news alerts or twitter timeline. We and Chicago are multi-faceted and often misunderstood. Read our stories and walk our city and you will discover find something incredible.

"When you grow up on these blocks, you're built for them.
Speak freely
Think wittingly
Stand up
In the big bad city -
Chicago."

AN
ETERNAL
MEMORY

BY ALEXA C.

A tranquil summer night at Buckingham Fountain with my family
The circular fountain was surrounded with golden railing
Water swiftly arose and reflected off of the enormous skyscrapers
Mixtures of pastel colors intertwined in the sky

The rapid wind rustled against the trees
Cars rushed by with hundreds of beeps
The flashing of cameras
Water gushing into the air like a volcanic eruption

Our glistening eyes watched observantly
Measuring each water spout
Making guesses as to which would fly the highest
We were mesmerized

The glowing mist shifted towards
Staining the pavement
We all took a step back simultaneously
Although it still got to us
Softly landing and kissing our skin like a blanket

I felt at peace as I calmly stared
Admiring the beauty that was before my eyes

At the end of the day we had not a single worry
But we did have
An eternal memory of a stunning summer night at Buckingham Fountain

---

Alexa C. is a thirteen-year-old girl who is sure of her herself in every aspect possible. She has grown up on the South Side of Chicago with her parents and brother Oscar. Her hobbies include playing sports such as basketball and soccer as well as being mischievous. She hopes to one day become an architect and see the city she loves progress. She is inspired by hard workers and people who strive to make a change for a better future.

MY
CHICAGO
IS

BY DANIEL D.

My Chicago is home to the best sports teams
The Bears, Bulls, Sox, Blackhawks, and Skyhawks
Loud, packed stadiums filled with crazy, die-hard Chicago fans
My Chicago is the city of the deep dish
Cheesy, crispy crust, bursting-with-flavor pizza
The city of the Chicago hot dog
Soft poppy seed bun with a tangy bam that hits harder than your
Auntie Pam
The city where peace is no more than violence
Home of Chi-Town steppin
My Chicago is music, home of the best artists
Like Chance, Kanye, Common, and G Herbo
Home of the deadliest mafia and gangs
My Chicago is HOME

Daniel D. is seventeen years old and grew up in the Chatham neighborhood on the South Side of Chicago. He would love to meet his favorite artist, Chance the Rapper, who is also from Chatham. Daniel has a disability called spina bifida and plays wheelchair basketball. His wheelchair basketball team has competed at the national level. Daniel wants to go to college to play wheelchair basketball and also hopes to coach it.

THE GHETTO'S ART GALLERY

BY ANONYMOUS

As 2:00 a.m. approached, I sent my friend a message to make sure that our plans were still on for the night. While I waited for his response, I got my gear ready. I put on my black North Face and quietly packed Rustoleum cans in my backpack. Most of them were black and chrome, my favorite. I put two meanstreaks[1] and a couple of fat-caps[2] in my pocket when my phone vibrated. I saw my friend and his older brother parked in the alley with the lights off. Carefully, I opened my window, hoping that it wouldn't make noise. I jumped out and left it ajar.

As I walked up to my friend and his brother, I could see the smiles that they held on their faces. I loved seeing the passion that they had for the art. We couldn't spend a day without writing our graff names on something. Walls, rooftops, freight trains, windows, dumpsters, even stop signs. It was "everything goes" when it came to what we wrote our names on besides churches, schools, and privately owned property. We might be vandals, but we have our morals and limits.

We spent most of our summer break sketching in our black-books[3], critiquing each other, and listening to E.C. Illa or Typical Cats. I was still fairly new to the game at the time so I worked mostly on my handstyle[4] and throwies[5] while they worked on wild-styles[6] and burners[7].

We drove along the Orange Line while we talked about some spots they knew about. These spots that they had carefully scoped out for a couple of days were visible from the Orange Line train. Some were rooftops, and some were backsides of buildings. Either way, I was eager to paint as it was my first time doing something that'd actually get some recognition. I

---

[1] Meanstreak- A solidified paint stick marker.

[2] Fat-cap- A spray can nozzle used for a wide coverage of paint.

[3] Black-book- A graffiti artist's sketchbook.

[4] Handstyle- A graffiti writer's unique style in his tag.

[5] Throwie- A quick and relatively simple 3D piece of a graffiti artist's name.

[6] Wildstyle- A complex form of graffiti that consists of 3D letters, a variety of colors, and lots of detail.

[7] Burner- A stylized graffiti piece of a graffiti writer's name which can be said to be a simpler wildstyle.

was referred to as a toy[8], but we all have to start somewhere.

We pulled over on a sketchy residential street and parked. I was already anxious as it was, and the unfamiliar area didn't help. I put my hood on, grabbed my backpack, and followed the crew. The lights shined a golden filter down the all-too-familiar Chicago alley: gang graffiti on the garages, broken glass on the rugged pavement, and a few dumpster rats, of course. Eventually, we walked up to the back of a tall building at the end of the alley. My friend handed over his backpack to me and scaled the dumpster that sat next to a window ledge. From the window ledge, he made his way up an unstable fire escape. We tossed our backpacks up to him and climbed up. At the top, I found that there were no walls. Instead, I came across rows of short banks that faced the train tracks behind us.

We were worry-free on the rooftop of the building. I could see the city's beautiful skyline in the distance. The lights at the top of the Willis Tower glistened like stars. In the air, the aroma of the Backwood my friend had sparked pierced my nose. The shaking of spray cans interrupted the whistles of the Windy City and we got to painting.

The following morning, we jumped on the Orange Line on Pulaski heading towards the Loop. All along the rooftops were pieces of graffiti. It was like the South Side's own ghetto art gallery. Most people on the train couldn't care less about the pieces of vandalism that surrounded them. When our pieces came up, we gazed with pride, knowing that that was our own exhibit.

---

[8] Toy- An inexperienced graffiti artist who is new to the scene.

SHE'CAGO

BY ISREAL B.

I still think she's beautiful
At times she isn't the cleanest under certain circumstances
Some people find love here, I guess you can call it romance
Some people come back to her
Some people don't get second chances
I still think she's beautiful
Being judged by the media
Kids don't play in her park anymore
Roses don't grow in her yard anymore
I still think she's beautiful
I see what they don't
I accept what they won't
The bad, the good
The fancy, the hood
The rich, the poor
Gaining justice and more
I can hear as she desperately cries out for help
Even when she's covered in yellow tape
I still think she's beautiful
I still think she's tasty
People might say she's ugly, but in my mind
I think she's beautiful
She'cago, Illinois.

Isreal B. is eighteen years old and from Chicago. She grew up in a large, loving household. Isreal hopes to graduate soon and become an entrepreneur and start her own makeup business. She enjoys poetry and deep conversations about life.

THE FERRIS WHEEL

BY ANAI C.

The sky was a deep shade of dark purple and the sun wasn't visible anymore. I could feel the breeze coming from the lake, even through my sweater. My family and I were standing in line to go on the Ferris wheel, which is one of the most famous places that Chicago is known for. The Ferris wheel had just been remodeled so we were excited to see what improvements were made. It had always been a tradition for us to go on it yearly. We have done this since I can remember.

Finally, it was our turn to get into the cart. I felt my stomach knot itself like when you're about to go on a rollercoaster. The doors were shut and we began to go up. As always, my mind was thinking up different scenarios in which something could possibly go wrong, I could fall to my immediate death. I looked out the window and we were suddenly already halfway up. I started to forget all those negative thoughts and replaced them with excitement!

When we reached the top, everything seemed so small underneath. The bright lights of the buildings looked like twinkling stars on a dark sky. The view of the skyline was breathtaking and so very beautiful. I felt a sense of calmness wash over my whole body and I was at peace. I know that's not something that's often heard of about Chicago, most things that are heard are about the violence and danger. That's not everything that Chicago is made up of, our city is also filled with beauty like on the Ferris Wheel. Of course I was taking pictures of the city because I am just like any other social media addict.

As we started to go down, I thought about how beautiful and unique Chicago is and how I sometimes take that for granted. Even though I had gone on the Ferris Wheel a hundred times, every time it's a new experience and it never fails to amaze me even more. Me and my family kept talking about our past experiences here and what we were going to do after.

The sky was now completely dark and the city lights were brighter than ever, almost blinding. It seemed like the more time that passed the more wonderful Chicago became. It is just one of the many things to love

Chicago for, it will never disappoint you. There is always something new to love and admire about this city.

As we reached the bottom, I felt a bit of sadness because it was already over. Those fifteen minutes now seemed like just a few seconds. When we got out, there was already another big line waiting to go in. The people smiled at us and we smiled back. On the way home, I was already bugging my parents about when we were going to come back to the Ferris Wheel. I couldn't wait to feel the excitement and adrenaline all over again.

Anai C. is a fourteen-year-old Hispanic girl who is in her last year of middle school at Jovita Idar Academy. She was born and raised in Chicago. She is a passionate guitarist and is obsessed with conspiracy theories (she especially believes that we are living in a multiverse). Her favorite subject is Lunch because she learns a lot there. Anai lives with her parents, three annoying siblings, two dogs, and fish.

THE
GIANT'S TRAIN

BY IXCHEL I.

Windy City, or Chi-town, whatever you call it.
It's a beautiful city despite some flaws.
Riding on the orange line all the way to downtown,
Seeing all the art on the buildings as they pass by.
I ride the train watching the city's buildings fly by
A blur of concrete, steel and glass,
Until my favorite approaches and the world slows.
A giant man sits on the side of a building
Watching over as the train passes by.
Sadness is furrowed on his brow.
Some would say he worries for the people he watches over,
The violence our city has gained a reputation for.
I disagree. I know that's not what crosses his mind.
The giant is a man of Chicago, and he knows the truth.
Like the Giant, Chicago is unique. The walls are painted
With the stories and characters of the city.
The Giant frowns not because he worries about us,
He frowns because he wishes the world could see what he sees.

Ixchel-Ix-zuhuy I. is a fourteen-year-old girl who goes to Jovita Idar Academy and has lived in Chicago all of her life. She enjoys playing basketball and 8Ball on iMessage games. By the way, she's really good. She also has a small Pomeranian named Pekas. Her favorite subject in school is Lunch (and Math).

HERE
IS CHICAGO

BY JAMIA B.

Imagine a world where there's always this immense dark cloud levitating over an entire city that feeds on the rate of crimes, cries, and the negativity that roams throughout the day. As dystopian as it may seem, this would be the city of Chicago, also known as Chi-town or the Windy City. Where I am from, but on-and-off raised, it's not always a bad place, but I personally wouldn't recommend it as a place to kick one's feet up and relax. Even the most beautiful part of Chicago has its rough days; it's a place where you just have to get in and get out, or it'll trap you like a foot caught inside a bear trap. It's a citywide virus that'll eventually start to spread more and destroy the good things that are left, such as the ability to venture out to different places, the ability to be free and not live in fear. Although I have never lived in the rundown, beat-up places where there are broken fences and abandoned buildings and homes—what some might call the ghetto—I still feel as if I have to be just as cautious because this is the city of Chicago. Here there are so many things going on with all of the violent crimes from A to Z.

Throughout it all, I choose to always think positive and to never get blindsided. I think about my younger self, back when others saw me as the quiet girl that never spoke up but made sure to do everything the right way--but not so quiet. I enjoyed how my life used to be before time passed me by, back when villains and superheroes were cool, when it was okay to let my mind bleed out what my soul wanted to say, when it was okay to show love and be happy without offending someone, when going outside didn't make me feel like I was a deer in a lion's domain, and having a dollar felt like I had ten. Times were better when I didn't need designer things to get looked at or loved.

Chicago wasn't always a bad place; it was the place to be once before the public created a twisted story for us to live up to and for outsiders to look at. And now that the future is here, it has us all in a headlock, suffering, struggling to find a way to make it out. The only way is for us to realize that we all need to come together as a city to be able to push through. I think Chicago will be great again, just when humans one day go extinct, with only the flowers and the sun to make it once more beautiful.

Jamia B. is seventeen years old and was born November 23rd in the city of Chicago but traveled around throughout her life from home to home with both her parents, two brothers and four sisters. Growing up, she loved to paint and sing, but as a shy, quiet girl, her voice didn't get much notice. This led her to change her songs into poems, which in turn led her to write stories about anything her mind desired. She loves everything about the writing process, from the plot twists to the stories that make you know her name to how she feels when she writes.

NEVER SETTLE, NEVER QUIT

BY DANIEL D.

Boom! Crash! Loud screams from all around. The ref blows the whistle to signal the end of the quarter. I was nervous when they blew the whistle but tired too. My heart was beating fast. I was sweaty and hot. Only twelve years old, and I was already playing in a championship game.

For what sport, you may ask. Is it football, or maybe soccer? No, wait is it baseball? It's none of those: It's wheelchair basketball, my favorite sport in the world. That championship game was during my very first year of playing when I was twelve years old. A social worker at the Children's Spina Bifida Clinic asked me if would I like to play wheelchair basketball. I had been wanting to try it for a while, so I said yes. I wasn't sure if I was going to enjoy it and keep playing, or if it was just going to be a one-time thing.

When I showed up for the first practice at Rainbow Beach Park, I was kind of scared. I walked in through the back entrance as they were about to start. I heard the sounds of basketballs dribbling on the hard wooden floor and the swooshing into the net. The other kids were getting into their sports chairs and messing around, shooting hoops, as they waited for the coach to start the practice. Of the twelve to fifteen players there, I didn't know any. But there was one person there who I did know: the coach. It was the same coach who had tried to get me to play when I was six years old. When I was a kid, I went to a park district summer camp at West Pullman Park, and the coach was good friends with the lady who was in charge of that camp. He came there to recruit players who were eligible for wheelchair basketball, and I was the only one there who was. Why would I play wheelchair basketball if I'm not in a wheelchair? I thought when he first mentioned it to me. I later figured out that you don't actually have to be in a wheelchair to play wheelchair basketball; you just have to have a disability. But back then I was only six, and I kept telling him no, I didn't want to play.

Flash forward six years later to when I was twelve, and that same coach was surprised to see me. My first practice was very fun. I met all of my new teammates, and they helped me learn how to shoot and how to push and all the basics of the game that I needed to know. My first game ever was on December 8, 2012 against the LWSRA Hawks. We had a great record that season and were in second place for most of the season and made it to the championship game in April in Louisville, KY. We took the lead in the beginning of the game but ended up losing the lead pretty quickly. In the end, we lost by nine points. I was pissed, but it was still a fun experience. That first year we grew as a team and we fought through it all the whole way. We became bigger and better and we just fell short, but we knew that the next year we would come back bigger, better, and stronger than before.

Daniel D. is seventeen years old and grew up in the Chatham neighborhood on the South Side of Chicago. He would love to meet his favorite artist, Chance the Rapper, who is also from Chatham. Daniel has a disability called spina bifida and plays wheelchair basketball. His wheelchair basketball team has competed at the national level. Daniel wants to go to college to play wheelchair basketball and also hopes to coach it.

A SOLITARY BLOCK

BY TERRANCE J.

I am from Latrobe, a solitary block that rarely gets hot. I am from a mother and a father in the home and a little sister and a big sister to assure I'm not alone. I am from fried cooked chicken and mashed potatoes on the stove—food that pleases the soul. I am from video game whipping to pancake flipping, down to milk dripping from the cookies that we left for Santa the night before the cookies grew stale like the tooth under my pillow for the Tooth Fairy, odd because they don't like dairy. . . because it stains the teeth that gives it a dreadful smell like stinky feet, so Febreze smelling couches beats "Chi" fish radiating around the room and sweat from hard work brings doom.

Terrance J. is a fifteen-year-old adolescent. Terrance's favorite place is his room. What he likes about life is that it has many experiences and twist and turns and most of all surprises. Terrance likes to play video games and chill. Terrance's hobbies are exercising and staying in shape. He is bold and he excels in math. He dreams of getting a masters degree someday.

MY CITY

BY DELTAH F.

City so amazing
How you've shaped me
I've dreamed, now it's time to build
Come see my city, my amazing city
Adventure awaits you, my active city
Gorgeous home of mine, misjudged and categorized
Outnumbered by surrounding critics plotting your destruction

The amazing city of
Mine

Deltah F. is seventeen years old and is from the Woodlawn community in Chicago. She enjoys spending time alone, sleeping, and hanging out with her friends. Her best friend is Meghan P. After she graduates, Deltah wants to go to school for cosmetology. She dreams of opening a one-stop shop for cutting and styling hair, doing nails, and other aesthetician stuff.

THE
FORGOTTEN
SIDE

BY LUIS C.

Colors:

Green, blue, red, purple

Orange, yellow, grey, black, white,

Colors splattered across the city

Spray painted all over the outside walls of everything

The outside wall of schools, stores, restaurants, demolition sites

Hollow things now bursting with life

Flyboy, South Ashland Avenue, Josefa Ortiz de Dominguez School

Cloud Gate, flamingo, Crown Fountain

Architectural masterpieces

Kanye West, Fall Out Boy, Chance the Rapper

All hailing from Chicago

Prepossessing, enchanting, opulent

Inspiring

Street to street

Museum to museum

Chicago

An artist's haven

Music flying in the air

The pride of each community

The shining gem

Chicago

Luis C. (eighth grade) is an eighth grader (duh) in Chicago whose hobbies include playing guitar, playing sports, reading, building things, watching Youtube, playing video games, and being overly sarcastic (notice how he didn't say writing). He is a giant nerd on many things including being weird, comics, Rick and Morty, video games, books, math, science, Greek and Roman mythology, believing conspiracy theories, books, and social studies (notice how he still didn't say writing). He is a Slytherin and says raccoons are his spirit animals. He has an awesome dog named JR (it's a Rottweiler). He has a dream of getting a PhD in something and finding Camp Half-Blood (even though that's in New York).

THE
STRUGGLE

BY ANGEL G.

The boy was never the type to give up on himself or on anyone else, always good-hearted, respectful, kind, goofy, and funny. People loved him. But, see, when he was seven years old, his father went to prison for a reason he really didn't know if he should believe or not, and the boy changed in a way he shouldn't have. He didn't know how to feel. That same good-hearted, respectful, kind, goofy, funny kid wasn't quite there. He still had a goofy side and was still funny, so he thought. Respectful? Not so much. When he started first grade back in 2007, he always got into trouble. He never really understood why he would act out, but he just did. People started showing him attention; he never really got that at home. Being the middle child of six wasn't really working out for him. He tried to communicate with his brothers and sisters, but they'd just bully him. Growing up, all he ever heard was, "You look just like your father." At first, it was usually his mother saying that, but then his brothers and sisters started picking it up and using it against him every chance they got. Eventually he got used to it, but it still hurt, so the acting up in school got worse. His teachers sent him to the principal's office nearly every day for disrupting the class and not turning in his work.

His mother tried her best to keep the family together. She was a strong, independent woman for a long time. But everyone needs love, right? So when she met a guy who showed her and her kids some love and attention, she let this guy move in with her family. That's when things changed. They would argue, and that's normal, right? But not when the boy heard his mother crying because this guy put his hands on her. To cope with the stress and disappointment, he started writing music, hanging around the wrong crowd, smoking marijuana, following his older brother and his homies' footsteps. They were the "cool kids," so that's what he wanted to be. Or maybe he wanted another kind of family to notice him. He didn't really know. He knows now that he made some mistakes and disappointed his mother, could see it in her eyes every time she had to bail him out of that police station on Cermak and Cicero. Over the years, the boy started arguing with his mother every night. Their relationship went south, and so did his grades in school. He never paid attention—he just became a class clown, the kid who wandered the halls and got away with everything even if he disrespected the principal. Since the boy's relationship with his mother wasn't great, he wouldn't be home much. He'd argue with her just so he could leave the house or have time alone to write music in peace. That was his comfort zone: music. He wasn't good at writing at first, but as he got older, everything spilled out of his heart.

The boy grew tired of seeing his mother getting beaten, and one night he stepped up to her boyfriend as he was threatening to hit her. That night everything changed because the boyfriend didn't take it well and wanted to fight the boy. The mom's boyfriend then began threatening the boy, calling him names and provoking him to fight. The boy saw his mother in a whole new way and realized she wasn't going to leave her boyfriend. By this point they had two kids together, and she was obviously scared to lose him, even though he was beating her. Something had to change, so the boy asked his mother who she was going to choose--him, or her boyfriend. Well, the boy is on his own road now, so you know who she chose.

The boy moved out of his mother's place and into his uncle's house. He's still pursuing music, and he loves it. He gets studio sessions from time to time, and he dropped a few songs on SoundCloud. That "wrong crowd" he used to hang with? They're all trying to stay alive because another "crowd" wants them dead. It's sad and isn't the life he wants, so he has a job and makes his own money. He's back in school, earning good grades and getting recognized with awards for perfect attendance and student improvement. When he calls to check on his mother, brothers, and sisters, she either answers or she doesn't, but at least he tries. He hopes for the best for his family, and he hopes his mother comes out of her shell and leaves that man so the family can be together again. In the future, the boy wishes to have a better relationship with his mother. He also hopes to be a famous rapper who helps people in need and encourages more kids to chase their dreams.

Angel J. G. is seventeen years old and was born in Chicago. He is a very smart kid, but he grew up in a rough environment, which caused him trouble in school. His favorite things to do are play basketball, write music and poems, take care of his family of 7 (not including himself). He is currently in a more respected environment and is doing very well in school. In the future, he would like to be a famous rapper and wants to influence other kids from rough environments and show them anything is possible.

MY
CULTURAL CITY

BY ESMERALDA O.

It was a dreary, gloomy day, as if to match El Dia De Los Muertos. We arrived at the museum as we do annually; the radiant colors seemed to pop out at me. The dark black contrasted with the glossy orange that seemed to be as loud as the sun. We entered the museum excited as hell (well, at least I was) to see the special exhibitions of the people that have passed away and that had an impact on the Mexican culture. After all, it was El Dia De Los Muertos which we use to remember important people in our lives that have passed away.

There was an exhibition that popped out the most to me; it was of the most important people that created huge changes in Mexico. To see these people stand up for something they thought is wrong, to stand up for a chance to make a difference, it made me realize that's what Chicago is about. We've recently had the March for the Dreamers which shows how together, we can come to make a big difference, and fight for something that benefits not only ourselves but the people we love and care about. This is my Chicago because we have people that have made drastic changes and improvements to our city. It's amazing to notice that both of my worlds seem to have things in common: they take care of one another as if they were family. People's experiences, memories, and history will forever be remembered in that museum as a way for our generation to learn about our ancestors.

Additionally, as a young Latina teen, I never understood the importance of my culture and heritage. But as my mom started telling me stories and urban legends such as La Llorona, or el chupacabra. I became interested in knowing more about my background. She told me that when she was a young girl growing up, she would always be walking around en El Rancho on those hot summer days with her cousins and siblings exploring their neighborhood. They would get into mischievous trouble and I just happened to realize I do the same thing with my cousins and brothers. Seemingly without noticing, this became a daily summer routine. Staying up late on hot summer days, going to 7-Eleven when we're craving food or just as a nighttime adventure. But what I can clearly remember from all those hot summer days would be playing soccer in the glistening sun while the cold rain drops rest on my sweaty, glowing skin. Honestly, the best part of all would be getting in trouble with my cousins and brother or having to climb fences to avoid almost getting caught exploring abandoned places. This created a form of connection with my mother to notice we had something of our childhood in common and that made my relationship with my mother stronger.

This museum made me feel connected to my heritage. More importantly, it made me proud of the Hispanic community in Chicago. What made me feel the proudest would be that, although this isn't Mexico, this museum gives opportunities for teens like me to learn more about back home (Mexico). Also, this can serve as a resource to the people that like to judge my culture without really knowing about it, a chance to see how great we truly are, not only as individuals but as a community. To know we are diverse in culture fills me with excitement to call this my Chicago.

Esmeralda O. is a fourteen-year-old teen who attends Jovita Idar Academy. She lives in West Englewood and has been living in Chicago since Day 1. She enjoys playing basketball, taking pictures of nature, and loves sleeping a lot. Esme aspires to one day play basketball overseas (or to at least be 5'8") but her expectations are too high for the moment. Oh, did I mention, she likes listening to Kanye West, Chance The Rapper, Biggie Smalls and old hip-hop hits.

NATURE
IN THE CITY

BY ALEXANDER C.

If you aren't from here you would think
Big city, fancy things, fancy people
A concrete jungle filled with technological dreams,
But what many don't see
And most cities don't have
Is the nature that surrounds us
Giving us an escape from the grind and grime.

Riding through the park
The route has become second nature.
The fresh fall air envelopes me,
Colored leaves float gently down from their branches.
For hours I ride, pushing to the limit,
Refusing to give up my piece of The Golden Country
For even a moment longer than I have to;

My city is a city where brick and grass melt together,
Concrete and trees, giving me the best of both worlds.

Alex C. is a student at Jovita Idar Academy. He is fourteen years old and has lived in Chicago his whole fourteen years of life. He loves to play music and he also loves to play video games. He is a really smart, funny, and great kid that has good grades. He owns horses and he also likes to ride horses in a way that goes with his Mexican culture. He's a young man who still doesn't know what he wants when he is older.

DEAR MOM, I DON'T MISS CHICAGO

BY PAOLA S.

She is six years old and lying on the floor with her mom in their sad, mostly empty living room. It's empty because they don't have any furniture other than the orange bucket she was sitting on earlier and a white broken plastic chair in the corner. Her mom is online dating and trying to find someone to connect with since she didn't connect with her father. She sits up and looks at her mom, so happy with her eyes locked on the crimson and black laptop screen. She can't see the girl staring at her, admiring her, because she is admiring another man.

They had just returned to their old house on California Ave after living in Texas since her dad kicked them out. They stayed for two years until her father started begging them to come back like his life depended on it, so they did.

Her dad stumbles in drunk. He had just gotten home from the bar. The young child scoots in closer to her mother as fear rushes through her body, like someone has spilled a bucket of icy cold water over her. As she makes eye contact with him, the girl knows he isn't just drunk—he's on drugs, too. Her mother sits up in front of her, almost like she knew what was coming. Her mother knew what he would do. Drunk and messy, he grabs a glass cup and throws it at them, yelling drunk nonsense. The fragile six year old is frozen with fear, almost like time has stopped only her body. As the glass makes contact with the floor, it shatters, and finally she is able to react. Glass flies and only strikes her mother, even though the glass had broken only a foot away from the child. Her mother has glass in her leg because she swiftly moved her baby out of the way. She's holding her with her arms and legs wrapped around her as if she would run away. The child could never tell how she were so prepared for all this. It's like her mother lived this before. Maybe she went through this before she met her father. Maybe she dreamt it. All she knows is that her mother is broken. She didn't see the glass as a cup she drank her juice out of this morning. She saw her mother's heart instead, shattered and broken, the million little pieces of it scattered around the empty living room floor. She looked at her mother, and she smiled and held her. Her mother didn't even cry. Not from what the child could see.

She is eight years old and it's December. It's almost her mom's birthday and Christmas. She lies in bed, thinking about everything and nothing. She can't focus on one thing because she's thinking about several other things. As an eight year old, the young girl is thinking about love. Does it actually exist, or is it just an illusion? Does it blind a person? Did it blind her mom, or does she even love her dad at all? She doesn't think so. It's currently 2 a.m. She's alone in the room she shares with her older brother, and she cannot sleep. The pitch black room swallows the child whole, and her eyes can't even adjust to the eerie darkness.

The silence is uncomfortable and disturbing, but it doesn't last very long. She doesn't know why she was expect things to be different—they never are. She was hoping he wouldn't even come home. He does. His presence is like a dark cloud rolling in. A tornado. Something powerful and dangerous. Their fear fuels him. He makes his grand entrance by slamming the door behind him.

She is now 17 years old, and just moved back to Chicago. Without her mother. This time, everything's different. Her mother is in the suburbs, and her mother kicked her out. Now, the girl lives with the man who did so much damage. Not just physically, but mentally and emotionally, too. She doesn't have a choice. Where else would she go? This is her last resort.

As she sits alone, in her big, empty room, she says to herself, she wishes to her mother,

"Mom, I didn't miss Chicago, and I still don't miss Chicago."

Paola Ruby S. is seventeen years old and was born in Chicago. She moved to the suburbs at nine years old and moved back to the city at seventeen. She loves makeup and loves the outdoors. She loves metal, rock, and alternative music. Her dream is to become a tattoo artist.

WRITING PROMPT 1:

Write a poem
or
make a list
where every line
begins with:

My Chicago is. . .

AUSTIN

BY CHASEON E.

Should I compete against all
Should I mess up to make y'all think I have a flaw
No one's perfect
I get no one's perfect
I know I wasn't no perfect child
I wasn't born with that perfect smile
My actions making y'all think that I'm wild
But this is above
My style is fly like a dove
I'm feeling pain but I'm d@#^ sure ain't stressing over love
This make y'all think of those raps from Cottage Grove
People whipping ghost-face on the stove
But I'm from sum different
I'm from sum new
I'm from that independent child that pay rent too
I'm from Austin
I'm from the West-Side
I'm from kids arguing over Kyrie going to Boston
I'm from drive bys
And watching ride along
To seeing kids saying they too young to die at all
But I see all better
I see good weather
I see kids in the future stacking legal cheddar
This is my story
This my verse
This is something that's worse than a curse
This is sum real
This is how I feel
This is something that's worth more than that drug deal

Or better yet people getting sum up for the kill
So put the guns down
This is enough
I'm tired of hearing kids saying they grew up rough
We are not perfect
I know that we not
We need to be the climax changing in the plot

Chaseon E. is a fifteen-year-old freshman who attends Michele Clark High School. He is smart, enthusiastic and well you guessed it, is short. He loves pizza but cannot eat it because of the fact that he's allergic to it. Chaseon is a deep poet/ rapper who also is a performer for his after school program BUILD. When he grows up, he wants to see just how much his words will affect the world.

BIG BALLER

BY ELIJAH S.

A late, cool, windy night, sweat running down my face. My legs feeling as if they aren't able to hold my weight anymore, feeling sore and weak. I pick the basketball up and shoot another shot into the net. My friend and I have been non-stop playing at McKinley Park. The street is filled with nothing but cars passing by.

Thirty minutes later my dad finally picks us up. We head back to my friends house so I can sleepover. I go to take a shower. Forty-five minutes later I'm out. We head to his room exhausted and sore, ready to knock out. I wake up to my friends dog, Hershey, scratching at his door. I open it and here she comes licking all over my face. It's a quiet morning, tired from the day before, we stay inside his room watching Youtube. We put on basketball. We finally get up and eat, brush up and head outside to play.

It's pouring outside. The cold rain hits my body and, at this moment, I'm ready to go back inside. He convinces me to go play and I swear I slip like four times. We play three or four hours in the cold rain. My hands are getting wrinkled because they're soaked. We're laughing and talking about things guys talk about: video games, girls, you know. Moments like this one are moments I'm going to remember till I take my last breath. We push ourselves to get better. Chicago's a place where people persist and are determined to reach their goals because you have people who put you down saying, "Chicago's nothing but a place where shooting goes on." When I play basketball, all I think about is getting over obstacles and proving people wrong.

We head inside soaked but I can't take a shower because I don't have any more clothes. We sit on his porch hoping that we'll dry off. We go back outside to play some more—we're soaked already as it is. We play until my legs are so weak that I can't possibly continue going. I text my dad to come pick me up. He shows up finally an hour later. I like it when it's just me and my dad. The car ride home is filled with laughter and jokes. He makes fun of me saying, "Once you beat me at basketball, then you're a good basketball player."

We stop at Wendy's to eat. I order three spicy chicken sandwiches and a large Dr. Pepper. Honestly, I finish it in ten minutes. It's a nice dry evening. When I get home I check my room and there's a brand new TV, PS4, and a bunch of games. I am thrilled. I rush to the shower taking fifteen minutes. That day without a doubt was the best day of my life. Knowing I was going to play basketball in the morning with my brother, I pass out exhausted. I wake up in the morning, brush up and head to the gym on my fixie. We play one on ones and five on fives for 4 hours. I go home and rest. Basketball is a no for a while.

I look up to my brother. I want to follow his footsteps. He's in the Marines and was on a basketball team. He's my role model and he inspires me to become someone better than I hope to one day be. I wanna go to the Marines and hopefully if I try hard enough, I can achieve my dream of becoming a professional basketball player.

Elijah S. is a fourteen-year-old boy who attends Jovita Idar Academy. He loves playing basketball and enjoys the competition and challenges it brings him. He's a big gamer and spends most of his weekend gaming with friends. At the moment his parents are divorced and he lives with his dad. His future career is to one day become a professional basketball player and to win a State Championship.

A CHINATOWN FANTASY

BY VANESSA H.

Chinatown pulls me by the arm
As my family and friends walk right past the market
Where I'm able to see fresh oranges, fidget spinners, animals walking around.
The busy streets of Chinatown,
People keeping their heads down, blowing cigarette smoke.
So I walk past that man with the cigarette as quick as I can
To get on the next train available,
But now I don't know where I'm going. But that doesn't matter anymore.
Oh wait, I just remembered I spent all my money.
So I couldn't get those ice cream rolls everyone is talking about.
How am I gonna get back home now if I have no one to call? I'll solve it.
Chinatown is a chill place to be at.
Never boring for me.

This one time, I was finally able to get those ice cream rolls and they were amazing,
I got the flavor Oreo with whipped cream on top.
I was just amazed and shook how often I go to Chinatown, about once a week.

It's a place where I can see the world differently sometimes.

Vanessa H. is fourteen years old and has lived in Chicago her whole life. She enjoys being on her phone and likes downtown. One decent subject she likes is math. She is inspired by her brother. She loves pizza and is always watching *Law & Order* on Netflix.

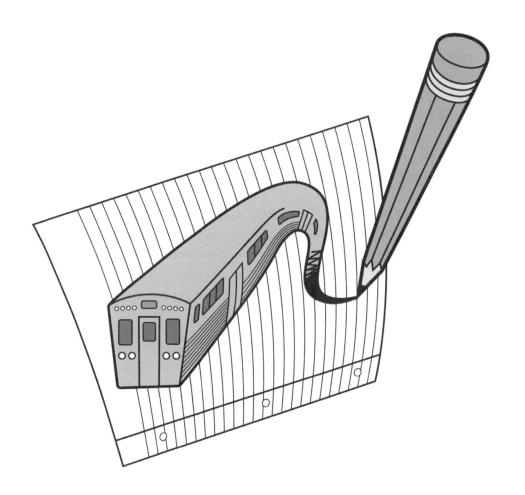

WRITING PROMPT 2:

Pick one to free write about.

A. What do you think Chicago's Ambrosia is?

B. Make a list of your favorite Chicago foods and where you get them.

MY CHICAGO MEMORY

BY BRIANNA R.

Growing up in Chicago has brought me lots of memories that I will always remember and lessons I will never forget. I have been dating my boyfriend, Jesus, for about three years now and I spend any day or night I can with him because being with him has become a daily routine for me. One afternoon, as I was coming out of school, the sun was boiling hot; I could feel my makeup melting. As I was waiting to get picked up by my dad, I started to feel nauseous and dizzy, but I thought it was just the heat affecting me. My dad had arrived in time to take me away from the angry sun, but I just seemed to feel sicker and sicker as the minutes went by. After the long car ride home, I quickly got out and ran inside to lie down in my room. As soon as I felt better, I called my boyfriend to tell him what had happened, and he agreed it was just because of dehydration. As the days went by, nothing seemed to get better. I still felt sick every day.

I went over to my boyfriend's house, and, as I was taking my sweater off, Jesus came closer, gave me a hug, and just stood there staring at me for a good two minutes.

"You're getting chubby," he said, with a blank face.

"I guess I been eating good lately," I replied.

I never realized it until he pointed it out, and the more I thought about it the more I started to feel insecure. My whole life, I have always been skinny and underweight. So, this felt weird to me. I ended up putting the thought at the back of my head and forgot about it. As days went by, I started getting chubbier. When the days turned into weeks and the weeks turned into months, I knew something wasn't right. I went over to my boyfriend's house and looked at him worriedly.

"What's wrong?" he asked. "You look like something's bothering you."

I took a deep breath.

"I just keep getting fat and I've always been skinny my whole life. Something just isn't right. My stomach is the only thing gaining weight."

"You thinking you're preg–"

"Pregnant. Yes, I do."

I looked at him, sad and scared, because growing up in Chicago I knew that every young girl who gets pregnant is judged and abandoned by the baby's father and her family. Several of my friends were already moms at that point, and as soon as their babies had arrived, they had no one around to help them. I hated the thought of only being seventeen years old and already becoming a mom. Being left alone was my biggest fear. To make matters worse, I felt sick to my stomach with worry. I felt as if my brain was going to explode when I thought of what was going to happen when I told my parents. I figured they would hate me and kick me out. Most of my friends who are teen moms in Chicago were kicked out as soon as their families found out about their pregnancies. I had millions of thoughts running through my mind. I had completely forgotten about my boyfriend standing right in front of me. I slowly looked him in the eyes, and he seemed calm. He looked at me, giving me a big smile and a hug. He looked me in the eyes.

"Everything is gonna be okay. I got you. I got us. We will get through this," he said.

I looked at him and suddenly felt so relieved that he wasn't going to leave me on my own. I was so happy, but I was still scared to tell my parents.

When I left his house, I stopped by Walgreens and bought two pregnancy tests. I rushed home and took them. I had to wait ten minutes, and the waiting was killing me. I just wanted to get it over with. After the ten minutes, I checked the tests. They were both positive. Once it was confirmed, I texted my boyfriend and knew it was time to tell my mom and dad.

I knew I wasn't going to be able to tell both of my parents face-to-face because I just didn't have the courage, so I texted my mom from my bedroom.

I have to tell you something, I sent.

Are you pregnant, she replied.

I was shocked. It was like deep down she knew what was wrong all this time. Just as I was about text her back, she came into my room. She had a blank look on her face, then suddenly she started crying.

"I knew it," she said. "Whatever you decide, your dad and I will be here to support you, whether you keep the baby or not."

Suddenly I felt like a really heavy weight was lifted off my shoulders. From that day on, I felt so much better knowing I had full support from my family and my boyfriend. Even though I felt good, I was still self conscious about what the people of my city would think about me, a seventeen year old, having a baby? People looked down on me and gave me dirty looks as I rode the bus. It was hard on me to not be embarrassed of how big I got each week and have everyone just stare me down. I hated how people would judge me right away without getting to know me. That's one problem my city has: everyone will be judged by somebody just by the way they dress, talk, and look. Despite the hate I would receive, I got happier each day as I followed up with my appointments. Each time, I had my boyfriend and sometimes my mom right by my side.

When I reached five months, the doctors were ready to tell me the gender of my baby. I was excited but nervous, and by looking at my boyfriend biting his nails, I could tell he was too. The doctor finally called us out, and we went into a small room and she started to put some sort of jelly on my stomach, and she looked at my baby with an ultrasound machine. After fifteen minutes of waiting, she was ready to tell me. She looked at me and my boyfriend and said, "You're having a girl!" I screamed with excitement. I just couldn't believe I was having a mini me! After we were done, we walked back home and I just couldn't resist the urge to tell my mom and family. I was ready to start everything pink. I arrived home and immediately ran to my parents and told them the news, and they jumped up and down with excitement.

Months went by and the end of September came closer. My due date, October 1st, was arriving. When October finally came, I had no signs of labor. I was starting to feel impatient, but everyone kept telling me to just relax and walk around to get the contractions started. Nothing seemed to happened and the day had already ended. October 2nd came and I felt like nothing was gonna happen either but I knew I had to relax and be calm. As the night arrived, I started to feel very uncomfortable and I kept tossing and turning everywhere.

5:00 a.m. came and I started getting really strong pain in my stomach every five minutes and knew it was contractions. I called my mom from my room and told her it was time. She quickly got up and told everyone to get ready. My parents rushed me to the hospital and then picked up my boyfriend. I was put in a room and the doctors gave me the epidural which was a needle inserted in my back so I wouldn't feel any pain. After that, my mom and my boyfriend came in the room and stayed there with me. After ten long hours I finally had my baby girl weighing 8 pounds and measuring 20 inches. I named her Sarahi Huerta Reyes. I was so happy and emotional that my baby was finally here after nine months. I knew everything was worth it, and I don't regret having a baby at a young age, despite the hate I receive from people and everyone who believed I wouldn't be able to handle it so young. My baby girl has come to be the reason I feel so motivated to finish school and get a job to be successful. I do everything for her and to try be a good mom who she will be proud of and whose footsteps she'll want to follow.

Brianna R. is a seventeen-year-old mom who lives on the south side of Chicago. She grew up in a loving Mexican household. She is a very outgoing person and loves her little family and friends, and would do anything for her daughter. She hopes in the future to become a cop and help her people.

LA
FIESTA
DEL SOL

BY MONSSE R.

"Hey, we're not going to find a parking space close by, just so you guys know," says my dad, addressing everyone in the car. We already know we're going to end up walking a few blocks though. We've lived in Chicago long enough.

It is mid-afternoon and the sun feels like it's boiling us alive, but instead of staying within the beautiful AC's range, we're headed out. We're going to La Fiesta Del Sol, a huge festival that hundreds of people–especially Mexicans–attend.

"Alright, get out," announces my father, as he finally finds a parking space just a few blocks away from the festival. Suddenly a chorus of complaints are heard.

"No…!"

"But it's hot outside!"

"I was listening to a good song!"

"I didn't even want to come!"

"Just get out!"says my mom sternly.

Out we go, into the blinding sun's reach and far away from the air conditioner. As we walk toward the festival, we start to formulate a plan. That way we can hit as many carnival rides and stalls as possible before leaving. We end up deciding to divide and conquer. My mom and I are one team and my father and two younger siblings are another. Also, because we only brought caps/hats and not sun umbrellas, we decide to stay in the close buildings' shadows.

My mother and I decide to go into the vendors' section before everything is sold out; my dad's teams go to the carnival section. As we walk I notice the buildings that surround the fair are ugly and decaying. They're falling apart and are heavily graffitied. It then crosses my mind that it's ironic that something so beautiful and lively–the festival–could be surrounded by something so disgusting–the buildings all around. It's also fascinating how the festival just seems to glow when compared to its surroundings.

As we continue to weave our way through the crowd, I can hear vendors shout out sale prices and weird, but friendly, slogans. The streets are packed and the sun is as strong as ever but nobody seems to mind. From the food vendors' stalls I can smell a mixture of steak, sugar, chocolate, pineapple, and just about every other food. Everything smells heavenly and everything is just about perfect. My mom and I go around sampling all sorts of foods, buying pina coladas (non alcoholic), and eating funnel cake. We also go around looking through stalls and find one that sells handmade bead jewelry. The necklaces and bracelets are gorgeous and incredibly well crafted. We end up buying a few bracelets simply 'cause we cannot resist jewelry. Time flies by and soon it's time to meet up with my dad's team.

When we do end up meeting with my father and siblings, it's a lot later, around 5 p.m. When we see them it's almost impossible not to laugh. All three of them are walking hand in hand carrying a whole bunch of stuffed animals and toys. Not to mention that both my siblings are carrying HUGE pina colada drinks. They're probably not even going to finish up the drinks! It amazes me to see that they were able to convince my dad to buy the drinks for them.

"Alright, let's go home," states my mother.

"No…!"

"I like it here!"

"Yeah!"

"It's too early to go home!"

"We're going home. It's going to get dangerous out here pretty soon anyway," says my mom, and that's the end of it.

We casually stroll through the thinning crowd and make our way out of the festival. From there we start walking towards our car. Once there my dad decides to play "La Vida Es Un Carnaval" by Celia Cruz. While sitting in our car, AC turned off and windows rolled all the way down, that an interesting thought hits me. The festival is, in a way, like the rest of Chicago. It's a single spot of beauty surrounded by overwhelming ugliness. It's shiny, glossy, beautiful new buildings surrounded by old, decaying, and abandoned warehouses. It's a spot of warmth in the cold.

Chicago is a flower blooming in the dark.

Monsse R. is a student at Jovita Idar Academy and currently lives in Chicago. She loves artists/musicians like Freddie Mercury, David Bowie, Gerard Way, and Frank Iero because "Heroes always get remembered but legends never die." She enjoys reading major series and trilogies like *The Maze Runner, Percy Jackson, The Hunger Games,* Harry Potter, *Divergent,* and *Miss Peregrine's Home For Peculiar Children.* Other interests include expanding her knowledge. She also enjoys dressing in weird and spontaneous clothing and reciting quotes and facts at random.

BUCKINGHAM
FOUNTAIN

BY DENISE C.

Birds chirping in the trees
People taking pictures
Leaves blowing in the breeze
People from different ethnicities in a large mixture
A big beautiful fountain splattering
Diversity with joy is all right here
People chattering all around
This big city is the place I call home
The love of my city just gives me cheer
Where you can never be alone
One special day
He feels worthy
To live on one more day
A tradition
To see the sun and moon go up
Filled with obligations
With merriment
He holds his cake, one bite with lots of frosting
Celebrating with Buckingham town fountain.
As he blows the candles
He says his wish
My home, my Chicago is here.

Denise C. is a fourteen-year-old who attends Jovita Idar Academy. She has lived in Chicago all her life. She lives alone with two lions, but she calls them her parents. She has two sisters–they really are lions. She has one dog, five cats, and two hamsters. Denise loves animals and wants to be a artist or a programmer. In her free time, she likes doing animations. She loves drinking Vivi boba tea while she works. She works everyday for her cats to have a better life. She likes to do art and her inspiration is Bob Ross. She believes Bob Ross is a god and good people die too quickly. Everyday she gives a moment of silence for Bob.

THE TIME I. . .

BY JANIYA F.

It was the summer of 2016. I was twelve years old and was riding my bike in front of my auntie's house on the West Side of Chicago in the Austin Community. I taught myself to ride a bike when I was ten. Even though I wasn't really good at riding, I taught myself the basics and that made me feel independent because I did it on my own.

So on this day, when I was twelve, I thought I was so raw, trying to do tricks, going fast, and standing up on my bike. Suddenly, I hit a crack in the pavement and flipped over the bike. I slid and my bike slid with me. I was in shock and my life flashed in front of my eyes, so I didn't feel anything. Everything was just numb. I got up like nothing happened. I took the bike to the backyard, ran in the house, and waited for my mama to call me to say she was outside. I got in the car and she said, "Girl, what happened to your forehead?"

I pulled down the visor and looking in the mirror and saw a big gash that was deep, showing my white meat. I started crying because my mom said, "Oh girl, you might need stitches." So we stopped at Walmart and got some gauze, ointment, and medical tape. We got back in the car, and my mama used bottled water and dabbed off the blood, put ointment on there with a Q-tip, and used two pieces of gauze to tape it down.

After my mom put the gauze on me, my auntie called asking if we were ready to go. Today was my grandmother's birthday and we were supposed to be going to 6978 Soul Food Restaurant to celebrate. We drove out of the Walmart parking lot and were on our way to the restaurant. When we got there, everyone was asking about my forehead because they saw the gauze. It made me feel a little embarrassed.

"You always think you grown," my grandma said. "Does it hurt?"

"A little bit," I responded. I really tried to enjoy myself and eat for the rest of the time that we were out. Later that night, I had to sleep on my back, which was uncomfortable because I'm used to sleeping on my stomach.

My mom woke up the next morning and I started in on my morning routine. I looked in the mirror and said, "DANG!" I had forgotten that I had a big piece of gauze on my forehead. It had stopped hurting so I hadn't thought about it.

My mom came in to change the bandage. "You messed up your face. You're going to have a scar for the rest of your life," she said.

She was right. I do have a scar. You can't really tell it's there, but I know it's there. It's like a small scratch on my forehead above my right eyebrow. When I see it, I think about that time I was teaching myself to ride a bike and I tell myself, "I should have never thought I was grown and tried to do tricks on a bike when I knew I couldn't." And I've never ridden a bike ever again.

Janiya F. is a fourteen-year-old student at Michele Clark High School who loves shopping, going out with her friends, and her mama. She was born on the South Side but was raised on the West Side of Chicago. She plans on taking college credit classes so she only has to be in college for two years and she looks forward to having her own apartment. She never thought about writing much before but has enjoyed it.

I
LOVE
CHICAGO

BY MIARA J.

I love Chicago because this is where I have lived all my life.

This place is where I learned everything.

I learned the ways of Chicago and I love it here because most of my family is here.

I love my life here because Chicago is unique.

There is no place like Chicago.

I don't think I could ever move out of Chicago.

My grandma is buried here, and I told her I would never leave here

And I'm keeping my promise.

She is my life; she's one of the reasons I'm alive.

She helped take care of me most of my life.

She made me who I am today.

Miara J. (Mia) is seventeen years old. She cares about her family and her friends. She considers herself a singer. She also plays volleyball. Her dream job is to be a chef. She's a really honest and funny person.

NIGHT LIGHTS

BY LUZ Q.

Many think Chicago's best view is of downtown where the "lights shine the brightest." However many don't know where the real Chicago is. . . . our own neighborhood

The moon was out and was shining at us, but our day wasn't over. All six neighbors came to my backyard to plan our next mischievous act. I was only nine sitting next to my best friend eating our lemon and gum palettas. Natalie and Evette were talking about their middle school stories as usual and Cruz was playing soccer with my brother on the dirty green grass. The night was almost ending and nothing came to our heads. Then, a few minutes later...

"Let's play cops and robbers," said my brother.

It was the perfect plan. It was our game we came up with when we were little. We snuck out the front door past our parents eating elotes and talking about each other's lives, ranting about something neither me or my friends understood.

We all paired up. When the guys starting counting down 10, 9, 8, 7 . . . Natalie and I ran like our life depended on it. 6, 5, 4 . . . We flew through the gates, sprang across the imperfect sidewalks, and jumped over the many fallen branches. 3, 2, 1 . . . We were far away from them.

It was 10:30 p.m. We looked back and saw the twenty different patterned houses we ran through. Some were boring brown, some were blue, some were broken down, some looked infamous. It was an absolute success. We ended by the corner store. My chest was finally out of breath and we decided to go inside to buy a few snacks. By our luck, Rosario decided to give us everything free. Everybody knew us here. We were the "twins" as they would say.

Five minutes later we were sitting at the sidewalk outside the corner store. We looked up and directly in front of us was the Chicago skyline with irrational building heights. We could see the whole downtown in a smaller version. We questioned how our city could be this beautiful. The lights combined on the buildings reflected brighter on us. . . We were complete champions, even if our knees were scraped, even if our hair looked like lion's manes, even if our mouths were full of thirst. Every "if" didn't matter. We were completly free.

The hot air brushing up my arm gave me a reposing sensation. The calmness of the night made me feel secure. Everything felt perfect at the moment. This was my city where I grew up, where I was able to live my childhood. It was my night light where I always felt glory.

Luz Q. is a thirteen-year-old currently attending Jovita Idar Academy. At the moment she is doing activities such as running, soccer, and dancing, although she's not really good at any at all. She hopes in the future to study criminology and become a detective to pay back and help her parents for all the sacrifices and support they have given their daughter.

COLORS ROAM
THE SKY
AT NAVY PIER

BY SAMANTHA M.

The stars shined bright in the dark night sky
My family and I rushed past the Ferris wheel at Navy Pier into a section
of grass
My mother placed a blanket for everyone to sit on
We were all ready for the show to begin, we were just in time. . .

A loud screech pierced our silent excitement
We looked up, an explosion full of colors emerged in the sky
The colors glowed and shined in the nighttime sky
Our eyes sparkled in amazement
It almost seemed like a new future began
with my family by my side

After every explosion the vibrant colors went off into different directions gliding down peacefully into the great lake
The sparkles float down slowly then another firework would shoot out
My family and I will never get tired of watching this endless cycle of
beauty
We all stayed to watch the colors roam the sky

I leaned my head on father's shoulder
I felt his warmth
I felt safe next to my family
It was like an invincible bond between my brothers, parents, and me
My family and I grew closer together as we all watched the colors
dance in the nighttime sky

Samantha M. is fourteen and she lives with her two brothers, her mother, and father. She is currently attending school at Jovita Idar Academy. She is an eighth grader who is working her hardest to attend Mother Mcauley High School next year. Samantha's hobbies are: drawing, painting, taking photographs, and sports like basketball, swimming, and soccer. She loves her family and tries to make as many memories with her loving family as she can. She is living life to the fullest and is excited for what life has in store for her.

MR. JOSE-MARIA

BY JENNIFER A.

Before I start, I want to acknowledge something: I am weird. There's nothing to be ashamed of. Even when I'm in public, that doesn't stop me from being weird. I dance in public at the beach very unskillfully, I walked straight into a window, I walked into a pole, I'm all around weird. Or I'm just really over the top...or obnoxious. Anyway, I'm not afraid to be weird and over the top here. Chicago has that certain vibe where you can be strange and not be judged for it. So I, as a weirdo, love that about Chicago.

One day, being a lazy person, I was sitting down on the bench at the Crown Fountain, gasping for air.

Quick little history lesson here: Crown Fountain was designed by a Spanish artist by the name of Jaume Plensa. Its purpose was to show the diversity of Chicago itself.

Sorry, lesson over, back to the story.

It was around 9:40 at night and I was so tired. I had walked all over Chicago. And do you know what a smart individual like myself decided to do? Wear flats! Round of applause, please.

We were waiting for our mom to pick us up so we could go straight home. The moon was high in the sky, the leaves were rustling, cars were beeping, and, to top it all off, there was the water from the fountain. I, at this point, was falling asleep.

Then, something caught my eye. This man across the fountain had this huge mustache. My family and I are in LOVE with Super Mario. We grew up playing Super Mario so, for this guy to have a mustache that look almost exactly like Super Mario's... I went into full fangirl mode.

He was very lean, and he wore a white shirt, black pants, and some weird looking shoes. Overall, he was average looking. For the time being, let's call him Mr. Jose-Maria.

He was walking around for a while and just doing his thing. I looked away for like a second and he had so many kids running after him. I don't even know how... I looked away for a second!

These kids were throwing water at him and he would return every water splash. Keep in mind, these kids were here before I even got there. He would try to outrun them but, there were six kids running behind him. Then, he fell. I cannot tell you how loud everyone laughed, himself included. I laughed, even though I had been sleepy a couple minutes before. I was so entertained just like everyone there.

He fell two more times but, the fourth time he fell, the kids tackled him, and even from the bottom of the pile, he was still throwing water at them.

We all had a good time.

That's what Chicago is.

Chicago is this place where you can be goofy, silly, and obnoxious and still be accepted. Chicago is a place where art is treasured. Chicago is a place where sports are valued. Where kids know how to have a good time. Where a good taco place doesn't go unnoticed. Here, talent does not go unnoticed. Even one as simple as keeping a mustache very clean and smooth.

Chicago is full of talent. You just have to stop looking at the negatives instead of the positives and you'll realize this soon.

Jennifer A. is a fourteen-year-old Latina girl who has lived in Chicago since she was born. She attends Jovita Idar. She was never a huge fan of religion but her favorite Bible verse is Lunch 12:10 and her best friend is a burrito named Boberto De La Torre. Her favorite place in Chicago is the chips section in Walmart, along with the ice cream section. Her best qualities are sleeping for a very long time, eating a lot, and believing in conspiracy theories. She is still waiting for her friends to openly come out and say they're aliens. She does not believe that Earth is flat or a sphere but the Earth is rather a donut.

DOWNTOWN
TRAINS

BY AHISHA M.

Way before I knew how to drive, way before I had a car, I would move around anywhere however I could. Working at a young age and attending school, you can't let yourself depend on anyone or anything. So I would take trains and buses anywhere I went.

At the time, my grandmother was still with us. After she had suffered so much in life and was still going through so much stuff, I tried to do what was in my power to make it a little better. I would take her to places and eat or simply go for a walk as long as she was distracted. She used to love very simple things like the colorful flowers. Every day, I would go sit with her while she was watching her novelas. She once said, "Quisiera ir a un lugar donde hay muchas luces que brillen igual de bonitas que las estrellas ya que aquí no se pueden ver," and I said to her, "Abuelita, yo siempre que agarro el tren, pasó por un lugar donde se ven todas las luces de la ciudad tan hermosas como las estrellas en la noche, un dia te llevare a comer tu comida favorita y nos iremos a ver las luces."

She told me that she wanted to go to a place where there was lots of pretty lights shining like the bright stars, then I remembered the train ride that I would take at night. It popped into my head and I told her that one day I would take her out to eat her favorite food, then take her on a train to downtown so she could see what I would see every time that I took the train at night. Just so she could have a glance at the beautiful sunset that would lay the last rays of sun passed in between the tall buildings. So on the way back, she could experience all the lights that came from everywhere to give this city light. Many things happened in our lives, so I never got the chance to take her.

Now, even though I drive almost everywhere I go, I still sometimes take the trains that everybody hates because they're filthy, they're crowded, or simply because they have other forms of transportation. Just so I can glance at the view she wanted to stare at. Just so I could have her dreams well pressed in me because that's the beauty that our city gives us. Doesn't matter how simple they are. Riding that train once in a while makes me feel my grandma close to me.

Ahisha M. is an artistic nineteen-year-old mom. She moved to Chicago when she was seven from Mexico and has lived here ever since. She loves music, helping out, and wishes to one day become a teacher.

I REMEMBER. . .

BY KEVIN G.

I remember when I was at home. It was early in the morning when something bad happened. It had rained all night and it rained a lot. So in the morning, my mom woke me and my brother up to our house being flooded. I was seven years old, my sister was two, and my brother was twelve.

The water was coming from some cracks in the floor and the wall. It got everywhere. Our floor was slippery and the water was tall, around two feet high. It reached up to my sister. It reached up to my waist, so I waddled from my room to the front door. So did my family. I stayed calm. She said that everything was fine. My brother carried my sister. My mom didn't know what to do and my dad was working out of state so he couldn't do anything. I tried to help but I didn't know what to do. On my way to the door I saw the furniture was wet and there was a bad smell. It was like a rotten smell. I saw one of my soccer trophies getting really wet. It was floating and I felt upset that I saw something that I worked hard for ruined.

That's when our upstairs neighbors helped us clean the water from the flood. They got buckets and started to take the water outside. One of the neighbors helped us close the cracks that were in the wall and floor. We went to their place because it wasn't too safe for my little sister. She was 2' 1" and the flood was pretty tall. We couldn't leave her alone so someone had to go with her. I saw that my sister was scared and worried. It felt good having people that helped us and cared about us. It was heartwarming and I was happy.

When all the water was gone, I remember my sister wasn't scared anymore, she was relieved. My brother didn't really care, he had a blank expression. He didn't really have a reaction. He was calm through the whole thing. I felt happy, partly because there was no more water and because we had people to help us. People that were there for us.

They helped us because we're close with almost all of our neighbors. We all knew each other very well. That's why Chicago's great. That's my Chicago: helpful and reliable. We all know each other. We look out for each other and we help each other. We are all one big community in Chicago. That's one of the many reasons I love Chicago. Chicago will always be my home and I am proud of being born here.

Kevin G. is an eighth grader at Jovita Idar Academy. He likes video games. His favorite video game is Fortnite Battle Royal. Kevin's favorite food is chips. His favorite novel is *Ready Player One*. He one day hopes to become a professional soccer player and he also hopes to make it far in life. He likes to make other people smile and he is a very positive person.

HABIT ON
HARDING STREET

BY LAMERIA R.

An addiction to the way it fed her lies
An addiction to how it eased her aching pains
An addiction to whatever was helping her cling to life
An addiction to clear her

Mind.

Body.

Her Soul.

Death was expected to be peaceful
Peaceful for those who respected it

An addiction to how much attention she was getting
Not physical but mental attention
All in her head she couldn't shake how unreal it was
Not loved by the people around her, she quickly searched for a new light
I watched from a distance as I saw the addiction take over
Ten dollars to close the deal with the enemy himself

Temptation.

Passion.

Promises.

An addiction that was eventually too much for her body to handle
An addiction that took control of her mind
An addiction that we all turn our noses up too
An addiction to the white horse, the clear stalker
He promised to protect me, he promised that I wouldn't get hurt
An addiction that wrote her a pass to judgement

Judgment.

Life.
Worth.

An addiction that was worth losing her life for
An addiction that set her free
Free from all the hurt struggle and pain
An addiction that knows no name
An addiction that has a face
An addiction that has no shame
An addiction that claims its prize
An addiction for a life
A life for an addiction

Lameria Jean R. lives in Ashburn. She is seventeen years old and loves pizza and chicken tenders. Her name is her mom and dad's name put together. She has seven siblings, four on her mom's side and three on her dad's. She is the second oldest. She loves to write and dance. Anything that has to do with art, she is interested in. She was raised on the West Side of Chicago. She graduated grammar school from Lionel Hampton Elementary. She is normally a happy and caring person. She loves animals. She wants to study journalism after high school and later cosmetology.

THE
CHICAGO
YOU DON'T
GET TO SEE

BY ANDREA E.

Living on the South Side of Chicago, everyone has an opinion of the city. Especially our current president Donald Trump, believing what's best for Chicago is "sending in federal help." With all due respect, Mr. Trump, we don't need your help! My Chicago is nothing like the one you've portrayed.

Walking outside, I don't have fear in my eyes, but a grin when I see my neighborhood. Looking forward to every summer, because I know I'll have the best block party in the city. All you can see on everyone's face is a smile. Every year seems like we become closer and closer. The years help our relationship grow. Watching the people I grew up with really makes me appreciate my neighborhood. I haven't only had fun times with my neighborhood, I've had memorable moments with them. Being able to count on them for everything. If it's not for a cup of sugar, it's for a shoulder to cry on when a relative dies. Or being able to count on them when I fall off my bike and my knee is bleeding. These are the people that make me feel like home and don't make me feel left out.

Remembering the memories I had, just being eight years old and walking around with my block. Hearing my neighbor who lives at the corner of the block say, "Hey I have an idea! If you guys race, I will give the winner a dollar!"

"Yes! Let's do it, so we all line up here and you," pointing at the man who lives on the corner, "have your hands out, and who ever touches them first wins," says my sister.

"Okay we can do that, so get ready and all of you. Stand there and when I say go, all of you guys run."

We wait for our neighbor to say go. "Ready set go," he finally says. We run like we have never run before. Realizing that our neighbor wasn't there anymore. We all had anger in our face.

"Where is he? He told us he was going to give us a dollar and he left! That's not fair!" said my next door neighbor. He was only mad because he was the one that won.

With a disappointed face we waited and couldn't stop thinking about how he tricked us. And to this day, I remember that as if it was yesterday.

Remembering all the memories I made in my neighborhood, not understanding why people get scared of entering my neighborhood. I don't see a problem in a regular neighborhood in Chicago. I don't see the danger. All I see is my next door neighbor helping me with a popped wheel on my bike or helping me buy chocolates so I could go to a school trip. Viewing them as siblings, not just as "neighbors."

Being able to see people from five, eight years ago, watching how everyone has grown. Being able to say those were the people I grew up with. Those people are not just my neighbors, but my family. I didn't just grow up with two sisters, I grew up with ten sisters and ten brothers; my neighbors are my family. Being able to count on every single one of them to be able to help me and give me advice like a brother or sister would.

Other people that don't live in Chicago shouldn't make assumptions about someone's home. Judging a city and not understanding its background and how it's run doesn't give you the right to judge it. I've lived in Chicago my whole life and never once have I been afraid of my hometown.

Andrea E. is a Latina who is fourteen years old. She is currently attending Jovita Idar Academy. She has lived in the South Side of Chicago her whole life with her parents, and her older sister Fernanda. She had seven fishes and two bunnies when she was younger. To this day, she's trying to figure out where they are. Her favorite hobby is talking, because talking is great and there's really nothing better to do. She also loves to travel, especially to Mexico, where she is proud to be from and can learn more about her culture's background. Oh also, Andrea uses the phrase "tbh" (to be honest) way too much!

THE
NEW
MORNING

BY JENNIFER M.

The sun has arisen
The day has begun
One busy city
Full of culture and new experiences
All kinds of music flowing by
With cars honking away through town
As traffic surrounds the shallow streets
The view of an outshining skyline up ahead
Street lights reflecting through downtown buildings
Lake Michigan on the other end
Art-like features from wall to wall
So unique and full of life
Color spreading
Given by the four seasons through time
From foggy views to winter dooms
Rising to humid days
Summer being the most spectacular
Laying by the beach
A fresh breeze through my hair
The smell of blooming flowers
All around Grant Park
Families and friends uniting as one
What better day to go outside
One city like no other
As the sun sets
The night has come
Loud sirens run by
As darkness joins in
While beauty stays within
That's life in Chicago

Jennifer M. is a Hispanic fourteen-year-old who is attending Jovita Idar as an eighth grader. She was born and raised in Chicago her whole life, still sharing her Hispanic culture from Mexican parents. Being the middle child, she has grown to share both roles of the youngest and the oldest. As she comes from a diverse community, music has always been a part of her as she plays both the guitar and the piano and sings at her church in the youth group. She aspires to travel all around the world and admire nature and beauty. Being able to accomplish any dreams she seeks like her family is her inspiration to move forward and become successful in life.

HIGH
SCHOOL
EXPERIENCE

BY JERMELE S.

It was the end of summer vacation after eighth grade graduation, and the young man had finally found a place to stay. He was about to start his freshman year of high school, trying to find his way in Chicago while pursuing an education. He was living in Englewood, trying to maneuver around and evade chaos and distractions. These things could derail him from goals and plans he set for himself to have a successful future.

His first day at Horizon Science Academy was rough. He woke up late and missed his school bus. Immediately improvising, he put on his new school uniform and started walking towards the CTA bus stop, where he would catch the 49 Western bus. While he was walking, he spotted a group of gang members sitting on their porch and their appearance intimidated him. He wasn't familiar with them personally, but he knew about them through word of mouth and pictures on social media. His heart dropped a little lower into his stomach with each step. Although he couldn't express what he felt on the surface because of what was instilled into him while he was younger, he couldn't deny the discomfort he felt. He kept a stiff, stern, and nonchalant face while walking, keeping his eyes locked onto the sun rising in the east to have another focus.

He felt their eyes lock in on him, glued to him as he walked by. Out of his peripheral vision, he saw one of the gang members stand up slowly. The gang member spoke, but the young man on his way to school heard nothing. Getting a bit louder, the gang member said, "Aye foe, where you stay at?" This made chills go up the young man's spine in spite of the warm weather. The young man kept walking, and the gang member, followed by some others, walked slowly from the porch onto the sidewalk.

The young man turned around, looking down at his shadow and feeling the hot sun beaming on his neck, and slowly raised his eyes in front of him. As the young man looked at the group of guys, not focusing on a specific one, a police truck creeped into a parking spot by this situation.

Although he felt a sense of relief, the young man's face didn't express it. Police officers climbed out of the car with a hint of aggressiveness.

Another truck pulled up with more policemen. The officers told all of the young men to turn around and face to the side of them.

One of the guys in the group was giving an officer a hard time and in return, all of the officers handled all of them more aggressively. The officers taunted, pushed, pulled, spit, screamed racial slurs, and yelled throughout the process of detaining the men. From then on, the young man felt he couldn't trust police officers.

The situation died down, and the young man resumed his walk to the bus stop. The chills that had previously gone up his spine suddenly disappeared. Standing at the bus stop waiting, he started to think about how the rest of his day would go. I really did not think my first day of school would begin like this, he thought, this is slightly disappointing.

Arriving to school late, the student headed straight to the front desk, signed in, and proceeded to walk to class. One of the school hall monitors noticed that the late student was lost and helped him find his classroom. The student walked into the classroom, feeling out of place, and the hall monitor spoke for him, explaining why he was late to class. Luckily, the first day of school included a lot of announcements and introductions, so the student didn't miss anything essential.

He made his way to an open seat, sequestered away from the other students, trying to keep attention away from himself. The rest of the classroom looked closely at the new student. The teacher glanced at him and tried to address him but butchered his name. The class giggled quietly, but soon after the laughter died down, the attention was back on the new student.

The other students in the classroom staring at the newcomer, talking amongst themselves. This young man stood out from the rest for many reasons: he was 6'1 with big feet, a stocky body frame, a moustache, a goatee, and a beard. He thought of himself as just another freshman, but he could already hear a couple narratives of him floating around the classroom.

"He swole as hell." "He probably a big softy." "He a creep." "He weird lookin'." "He ugly."

A wave of irritation and disgust washed over the young man, but he swept it aside, trying not to let it bother him. He knew that being bitter about what another person said wouldn't help him or his goals. But him not responding to their comments only confirmed the narrative of him being "a big softy" in their eyes.

Throughout the day, people kept talking, staring, looking, harassing him. The teachers did not make it any better, saying that he looked like he was in his mid-thirties, to which the students laughed in agreement. In an effort to turn this into a positive thing, the student chose to think of himself as a celebrity, with all the other students giving him this unnecessary negative attention. This helped him process and digest the day to get through it. By lunchtime, he had stopped paying attention. For the rest of the day, it was nothing but a repeat of the first half of the day.

The end of the day approached. This initial high school experience opened his eyes to the types of people who exist in the world. After this day, he wanted to drop out, hurt a couple people, and just be done with life. Even though he wanted to give up, his infatuation with gaining knowledge--whether it's knowledge from the books or everyday experiences--helped him stay in school.

Jermele S. is seventeen years old and lives on the Southwest Side of Chicago. He moved from Belize at a young age. He wants to go to college to pursue a career in physics/engineering. For now, he likes to help produce and make music and meet new people. His dream is to be financially stable and meet beautiful women.

A FRONT ROW SEAT

BY EDGAR M.

Take me out to the ball game, take me
to the crowd.
One of my most favorite things
about Chicago is their baseball games.
Seeing the White Sox play in their league,
it always makes me excited to see who are they against.
I'm used to watching baseball games.
When I was younger, me and my whole family
would always go to the Sox games.
When my dad used to work at the factory,
his boss was the best-
he always gave us Sox game tickets.
We would not go in the car because
their parking is always full,
so we took the bus or the train.
I don't know how describe this place,
it's huge.
It feels like I'm inside of an alien ship.
Anyway, sometimes when we get tickets it's sometimes
front row seats.
We would see that home run or out of the park.
I got a autograph by one of the baseball players.
I have it hanging in my wall to remember the day I met a famous Sox
player
so we can keep the White Sox spirit.
We would get our White Sox shirts and jackets.
That's what I love about my
Chicago, this is what my Chicago means.
I don't care what they think.

Hopefully, in the future, my sister
can show her kids our childhood or

in the future, if I have kids of
my own, I can show them
where I used to go when I was
younger, where my family and I will go.
Thanks for understanding what
my Chicago means to me
from my own point of
view.

Edgar M. is a fourteen year old at Jovita Idar Academy. He has lived in Chicago his whole life. His favorite place to go to is downtown Chicago. In the future he wants to do blogs to keep his YouTube channel up, be famous, and make his family proud. The high school he wants to attend is UIC College Prep. His favorite cartoons are *Rick and Morty, The Simpsons* and *Family Guy*. He is a fisherman.

THE
ARC WITH
CULTURES

BY NINEL A.

It was an extremely bright and special day. I was riding in my car ready to make a stop. A stop that I didn't know about. I hopped down, excited to see what was waiting ahead of me. I saw many people with their electronics. They had some huge and bright smiles on their faces, almost as big as the sun.

However, I still didn't know what the surprise was my parents had planned on showing me. I wondered if it was or wasn't the surprise I was expecting. I looked around but I didn't see no Barbie doll dressed up in a charming beautiful dress with some sparkly high-heels.

As I made my way through so many smiling people, I saw this giant thing. It looked like a bean, which many people were taking pictures of. It turned out to be that my surprise wasn't a cute little Barbie doll. It was this giant bean. It was big and shiny. It had this giant curve in the middle which many people would pass through. My eyes were amazed with it. I now was able to understand why everyone was smiling with joy. I stared very closely into the shiny bean. I was able to see the sun reflecting its brightness. Then something even brighter than the sun caught my attention. It was a small girl who looked like a two or three year old. She was smiling and jumping along and clapping her hands.

In that moment I realized how much Chicago is worth and how lucky I am to live in Chicago. Chicago isn't just a 'weird, and violent' city, it's a place where joy and happiness occurs. It's a place where people are united. It's where you create the most amazing and unforgettable memories. It's a place that makes you feel like home. If you are feeling down, Chicago can give you a bright shiny smile with all these amazing places. Seeing a young little girl smiling means a lot. It means she was delighted with what she is seeing or doing.

Feeling proud of saying that I live in Chicago isn't something common. My Chicago has many fun places to visit. For example, the Sears tower, also known as the Willis tower. Along with its museums. My Chicago is famed for its bold architecture. One piece of architecture that stand out to me the most is the Little Village arc. This arc is meaningful because the way it says "Welcome to Little Village" is like how Chicago welcomes people into this beautiful city. Passing this arc, you can see many different cultures people bring with them. One of the most common culture that many people bring into Little Village is the Mexican culture. The food is amazing and unexplainable, especially when the hot sauce on the tacos hits your tongue and spices it up. I feel like the Little Village arc is what really represents us, the Mexicans, Hispanics, and Latinos.

However, there are many negative thoughts about Chicago. These thoughts people have about Chicago aren't even close to what Chicago really is. My chicago is a place where many dreams come true. Chicago and it's places give me strength to wake up each morning. My Chicago is part of my heart. Give it a try and it won't let you down. My Chicago is my inspiration!

Ninel A. is a student at Jovita Idar Academy. She has lived in Chicago her whole life. Ninel enjoys visiting new places with her family. Ninel lives with her three sisters and her inspirational parents. Ninel hopes she can travel to many places like Paris, etc. Ninel hopes that one day she can achieve all her goals.

WHAT I FEEL
ABOUT CHICAGO

BY SHARONDA J.

I love Chicago because I have a family there. Not just my blood family, but my community family. I love Chicago because I learned that what I the hate most, I love dealing with. I love Chicago because they have the best Italian beef and french fries. Warm weather in the winter, the packed beaches and pools in the summer. I love Chicago because it's where I belong.

Chicago makes me upset when I can't depend on it's people when I need them. I hate how our crime has increased, but it's more younger people committing crime. How every drug dealer on the corner tries to holler at you. I hate how my mom thinks it's me being mean but they piss me off at my school. Chicago makes me mad when they don't show their full potential.

To me, I think Chicago is getting worse. Chicago isn't how it used to be, we used to have fun late at night without getting hurt. Stay on the front porch and know that you're safe. Now we have to go home straight after school. The police don't protect us how they should. But as our generations come up, we will make a change.

Sharonda J. is a ninth grader at Michele Clark High School. She was born the day before the Fourth of July and she enjoys her birthday every year. She loves to dance, and it's her passion. She wants to be a neonatal nurse and have a celebration party. She loves all types of music and she can dance to all types of music. She is the best counselor you can talk to cause she been through it. She loves sherbert ice cream and if she is not in the mood or not being herself, give her Italian beef or chocolate. She will be happy in seconds.

WINTER
IN CHICAGO

BY MELANIE A.

Lining up to get ice skates and seeing families come together. Skating in downtown Navy Pier. Seeing parents putting on their children's skates while waiting in line, then beginning to skate. Followed by feet crying and arms screaming. But in the end laughter and happiness took over.

I soon realized how skating can bring people together and how strong everyone is. I saw that no matter what might be happening in their lives or what hardships they're going through, they can set that aside and come together for a day and celebrate Winter Wonderfest.

In the front of the line I saw family, friends, and lovers skate. As if nothing else mattered and they were the only people in the world. Everyone skated and when they did, the feeling of the world melting away began to emerge in you. Because everyone seemed so happy. There was no fear, no sadness, or anger. The only thing showing in their faces, in their eyes, was love and happiness. Everyone or everything was at peace, even if people were falling. At that moment, I saw beauty in Chicago. I saw how the people could form part of a beautiful painting representing Chicago, and in that painting there were all different colors with different faces but everything was formed together to create a moment that I will never forget.

Once I began to skate and fall, I grabbed onto the rails. Then I realized I wasn't the only one. Others were also holding on for dear life. They weren't scared though, they weren't angry either. It was strange how they were laughing. Some people were laughing so hard that it brought tears to their eyes. Yes, some were falling but they would get up and they were laughing. And no one was laughing at them, it was more of laughing with them, and once they got up they would fall over and over again. Yet no one was angry. No one cared that others saw. They were too busy enjoying themselves, too busy spending time with their families or friends to notice others looking at them.

And it made me realize that no matter how many times people would fall they would get back up. And not just in skating, but in life. Chicago, stand right up. Chicago stands tall with pride. The skyscrapers stay strong even after a blizzard, even after thunder and lightning. No matter the weather, no matter the tragedy that might occur, Chicago holds up its head with pride and stands strong just like its citizens. No one will ever see a skyscraper lying on its side looking as if it was about to fall. If it were about to fall then a group of people would come together, pushing, fixing it to look perfect. They will give it their all. All blood, sweat, and tears would be put in. That also implies for the community in Chicago. You will never see a person fall and everyone around them doing nothing. Blood, sweat, and tears will be put in so that no one or thing will be leaning to fall.

When I finally get off the ice my feet crying and my arms screaming, I first realized how much pain I was going to be in tomorrow. Secondly, I realized how I'm laughing and I'm not that angry. If anything, I don't think that I have ever laughed the way I did that night. I had never laughed that loud or that strong before.

Melanie A. D. is a fourteen-year-old Latina girl who has lived in Chicago all her life. Her favorite hobbies are creating music, reading, and writing. Although she can't spell. She suffers from a curse called the MAD curse. It makes everyone near her unable to spell properly. Most of the time she spends time questioning life and existence as it is. She was born on March 17, 2004.

EXPOSED TO THE WORLD

BY ANONYMOUS

Once I was very bad towards my parents, and in this situation I kinda lost a part of me that I believe I left behind when I was a child. But I also know that, in this situation, I was exposed to the world too young and couldn't nobody shield me at that time from my own self-destruction. I believe this day was when I was eleven. I was upset about something and I was over at my father's house. I was mad and I kinda just left and went out trying to discover why the world they was shielding me from was so bad. What I saw in this world was a little too much for me but at the same time I felt like I could have handled it but truly I couldn't, not by myself.

I truly love my father but my mother is different. I feel somewhat bad for her cause she wasn't able to do what she wanted to do because of me. I blame myself instead of the true person I need to blame for her missing out on her life. Cause she was too young to have me so everyday I fu** up, she regrets me more, I think. Sometimes you have to do what you need to do in order to survive but sometimes you have to let go of what your dreams are. See my dreams are to die sometimes to give back what she lost so that she would be to be able to pick her own card instead of the card she was dealt because she wasn't dealt the right card because of me. See I do love my mother, but not always and not forever.

Now on to my father. My father is the best person ever 'cause from him I learned to be careful of my decisions and choices that I make when it comes to family and to love those who love you and don't love who doesn't love you. I also learned to trust those who trust you and to keep an eye on who doesn't trust you cause you can't trust them. I find it hard to know who trust you and who don't.

Sometimes I hate my own kind. Sometimes they just love to make fun of their own kind. Yes, I know, "How can you hate your own kind?" Well in my own eyes, if you have something that they don't and they want it, they will either steal it or kill for it. See we hate being told that we do this unless it comes from our people but let me tell you something if you became a killer or a thief make sure you don't have a heart that's the only way we keep it moving. See I tell the truth when I write because I don't want people finding the truth about me. See my people are only very intelligent when it comes to our benefit. To be honest, I want to be something else when it comes to me. I want to be a killer but for the right things. See I like the color of red and black . I call myself bloodthirsty. Do you know why I can't stand when people tell me to watch out for me and my sibling? It's because as I keep going I'm gonna grow stronger and the stronger you get the more thirstier you get and I'm gonna teach my sibling to be less heart full and be more hurtful.

EXPELLED

BY HANNAH H.

In September 2015, I started high school at the Chicago High School for Agricultural Sciences. Everything seemed good for the first few months until I got sick. I was already on a 504 Plan from my middle school for my debilitating migraines. I first started to get really sick again in November. I had played basketball since fourth grade and played on the basketball team at CHSAS for a short period of time, but when I missed two days of practice while I was home with an excruciating migraine, I was kicked off the team. As much as I wanted to play basketball, I knew it was no longer an option due to my chronic migraines. I let go of basketball quickly, but my painful migraines continued, and I kept missing school often and falling behind on my work. Some teachers helped me catch up, but others just yelled at me for missing so much school.

I was in and out of the hospital constantly for my migraines, and all the doctors and nurses knew me well. When we would walk into the lobby of the hospital and a nurse we knew was doing check in, she would always take me right back to the the emergency room. I always brought doctor's notes to school to explain my absences. The first time I missed a few weeks of school in a row, the counselor pulled me out of my eighth period PE class. She walked into the classroom, looking like a creepy old librarian in her glasses and pantsuit, and glared at me.

"Hannah, now," she said in an annoyed tone.

Terrified, I grabbed my bag and followed her to her office, where she called my parents to let them know I was talking to her. Her tone with them was kind and friendly. After she hung up the phone, however, her demeanor changed abruptly to angry, which made me nervous. I had never gotten in trouble in school before, and I was already in trouble in my first few months at this school. I sat down in a chair next to the clock while she stayed standing, talking down to me.

"As a freshman, you can't miss this much school," she said with a scowl. "You're going to fall behind and fail, and then you'll have to repeat your freshman year. You won't be able to succeed after high school if you keep doing this."

I'm a failure. Everything sucks. I can't do it. It was stupid of me to even try. I tried not to cry as the thoughts swirled around my head, which was already throbbing with pain. I knew that as soon as the bell rang at 2:53, I could get out of there. I watched the clock tick 2:51, then 2:52.

"Where have you been?" she asked, glaring down at me.

"In and out of the hospital," I replied nervously.

"And what do the doctors say is wrong with you?" she shot back.

"They have no idea what causes the migraines," I replied. "They're constantly adjusting my medication, and sometimes I'm in the hospital for weeks at a time."

The bell finally rang, and I fled from her office, running to my locker as fast as I could. As soon as I left the building, I got into my mother's car and immediately broke down in tears. I had no control over my mysterious illness, and I was getting in trouble as if I did. I was so upset that I caused myself to get a migraine and didn't go to school for the next week. I was admitted to the hospital, and my parents decided to switch neurologists. At this point I had three MRIs, an EEG, a CT scan, and more x-rays than I could count. Whenever I went to the hospital, they put an IV in to keep me hydrated and medicated. I remember the feeling of the sharp needle piercing my skin while I held my breath and looked away. Whenever I got an IV, they always took my blood right after they put it in, because after so much time has passed, you can no longer get blood drawn from an IV. A week after I was released from the hospital, I went to my primary doctor for a regular follow up and a referral for a new neurologist. Later that week I saw the neurologist. She went over my medical history and noticed something was off with my blood pressure, so she ordered a tilt table test. That would take place in a couple of weeks, but in the meantime I tried to go back to school.

Unfortunately, that didn't go as well as I had hoped. As soon as first bell rang, the morning announcements began, and I was called down to the counselor's office. I already hated being at school, and my day had just started. As I walked into the office, I began to shake in fear, knowing that this would be the worst visit with the counselor yet.

"You missed too much school!" she yelled. "You'll have to do summer school."

I was upset, but I still believed I had a chance to catch up. As soon as I left her office, I texted my dad to come pick me up. After that I stopped going to school again. After a few weeks, it was finally time for my tilt table test, which I was nervous about because I didn't understand what was going to happen. As the test began, I started to lose my vision, then I heard ringing in my ears. I didn't know what was happening, so I asked the doctor to stop, but I had another few minutes left on the test. After another twenty seconds, I blacked out and started to seize. As scary as this was, it solved my medical mystery. I actually don't remember the seizure, but the doctor said that was normal. It was still terrifying to know I had a seizure.

I was diagnosed with orthostatic hypotension, which is a fancy term for low blood pressure. I was also diagnosed with cluster migraines, which is when migraines cluster together and last weeks before the pain goes away. The cluster migraines and hypotension together explained all my symptoms. It felt great to know what was wrong with me, but the new restrictions I had to live by upset me. Any sudden drop could cause me to seize, stroke out, or have a heart attack, so I could no longer go on roller coasters at carnivals or amusement parks. I also had to be careful at water parks with tall slides and sudden drops. Although I had mixed emotions about my diagnosis, I knew my life was changed for the better. With this new diagnosis came the haunting thought of returning to school.

At this point I was being bullied not only by the school counselor but by my stalker, a girl who made me hate myself. I knew this girl in middle school, but she didn't become a major problem until high school. She would show up at my house randomly even though I never gave her my address. The school did not see her as an issue, so they wouldn't help me. I became depressed and avoided school and social encounters as best I could. After a while, I began to consider a different option: suicide. I didn't try, but I thought about it for a long time before I finally went through an outpatient program at a hospital to help me get better. As soon as I finished the program in April 2016, I had to go back to school, where I was forced to be in many uncomfortable situations. I had panic attacks and was asked to stay in the corner of the room during them so I would not disturb the class. Being at school made me feel even worse, so I stopped going altogether. I went to summer school and passed, but by the time fall came around, I started missing school again.

"If you don't get your act together, you'll be kicked out," the counselor informed me.

I started to go to school again. The day before Thanksgiving break, on November 22, 2016, a security guard and my dad walked into my fourth period class. I was told to clean out my locker, leave, and never come back. I was supposed to be protected from being kicked out under my 504 Plan, but the school didn't care. They put me on the waiting list for an alternative school, Pathways in Education, without my parents' permission. Being kicked out of school right before Thanksgiving was difficult, as I knew I would be surrounded by family for the holiday. I didn't tell anyone in my extended family about getting kicked out, and I managed to avoid telling them for seven months. Unfortunately, I did have to tell my friends, who wondered why I wasn't in school anymore. I was really upset, and my friends didn't know how to react. I later found out that teachers at my old school used me as an example.

"If you don't want to end up like Hannah, you need to do your work," one teacher said.

It hurt, but I started a new school and made new friends. It wasn't that easy at first, though. When I started at Pathways, I was terrified. It was a new environment, and I wasn't good in social situations. My teacher would say good morning, and I would immediately back off. I was polite and said good morning back, but he could tell I was uncomfortable. I was like that for about six to seven months, until I started a personal finance class and began to make friends. Then I took an English class, where I was put into a group of people who would soon become some of my best friends. Being at Pathways has greatly improved my social skills, and I regularly attend school. I still suffer from migraines, but they are much more manageable now. Everything that happened to me got me to where I am today, and I know that I am supposed to be where I am now. I have friends, I'm going to school, and I'm no longer depressed. This has given me a chance to go to college after I finish high school, something I didn't think I would be able to do. I am a better person because of my experience.

Hannah H. is seventeen years old and grew up in the Beverly-Mount Greenwood neighborhood. She loves to hang out with friends and enjoys spending time with family. She has one sister who is two and a half years younger than she is. She also loves to play with her German Shepherd whose name is Zoey.

MY HAPPINESS

BY JASMINE B.

Chicago is a sort of miracle

A city

A plan

A place where authorities and institutions greet

A surprisingly strong cultured city

Where groups come together

A glimpse of happiness

Where my happiness comes from church

It's a place where I go when I'm down

'Cause it feels like my home

My church is really big, you see tons of people go

Different race, tons of activities, different helping groups

It's a. . .

A cluster

A growing group

The reality of Chicago exists

Jasmine B. is a student at Jovita Idar Academy. She is thirteen years old and she has lived in Chicago since she was born. Some of her hobbies are volleyball and she loves to do makeup. She is a girl with a huge family (two sisters + two step sisters + one brother + two step brothers+ her). One of her favorite subjects is math. She would like to take a trip to Cancun for her quinceanera. She is striving to be a nurse or doctor later in the future.

PIZZA
MY HEART

BY DANIEL R.

March 28, 2010. It was a brilliantly bright morning in Chicago. My father was driving my family and I to Connie's Pizza- one of the best pizzerias in the city. As my dad was driving, I'd noticed that my family hadn't spoken a word once in the car. So, as a curious six-year-old, I started to ask my dad questions to break the silence. I asked, "What's so special today that we're heading to Connie's?", but all he replied was, "Figure it out," so I thought about it... somewhat hard until I remembered, it was my parents anniversary!

From a distance, I saw a fairly large sign, and on that sign in bright red lettering read "Connie's Pizza". I looked around the car and saw the relieved face expressions my family made once we finally arrived.

We parked right in front by the entrance. Once we got out of the car, we started to head to the entrance. Inside it's a whole realm of nostalgia, taking you back seventy years to the Forties. Connie's is also a great place to see a wide variety of ethnicities come together to feast with their family, and I wasn't surprised to see Connie's filled with a variety of people. We waited until the hostess guided us to a table, which she did after it took her about eight minutes to realize we were there.

The hostess sat us in a very vacant area filled with pictures of old-timey Chicago. The waiter started to approached our table. He was a very tall young man, and he asked us what we wanted to drink. I ordered a lemonade, my dad ordered a water, my mom ordered Coke, and I forgot what my sister ordered. The waiter finished writing and I looked over the menu and the thin-slice sausage pizza - one of the best items that is offered on the menu- caught my eyes. The waiter arrived with our drinks with his medium-size notepad dangling out his pocket. He gave us all of our drinks one by one. Once he finished he took out his notepad and ask us what we wanted to order. My dad ordered a deep-dish pizza (Chicago's best specialty) with sausage and mushrooms on top. Then I ordered the thin-slice sausage pizza for both my sister and I. The waiter put the drinks down and went into the kitchen.

Once the waiter finished writing the orders down, my dad called him over. He was whispering into his ear. They finished talking after about twenty seconds of talking, and the waiter returned to the kitchen. We waited for about forty-five minutes for the pizza to arrive. During those forty-five minutes, my dad and I had a whole conversation of the memories he and my mom had coming here when we were little. He told me that he wanted to show my mom some of the best pizzerias around Chicago and they came across here. The conversation lasted around thirty-eight minutes with the rest being awkward silence. I was relieved when they finally came, and once I saw the pizza my mouth started to water. A steaming Italiano Roman style flatbread, layered with thick and rich tomato sauce, topped with amazingly delicious sausage as the pizza topping. Shredded mozzarella cheese is better than nothing. Pizza calls hungry hordes for coverage. I started to dig in after the waiter was finished placing the pizza on our table. The pizza was amazing. The pizza had the right amount of sauce and cheese proportions and the sausage was evenly placed on the pizza like they used a ruler. Connie's was packed to the bone at this time. People from all around Chicago came here to spend their Saturday afternoon with family and friends at Connie's.

I finished feasting. My whole meal consisted of 78% of pizza and 22% of lemonade. Five to seven minutes after I finished eating, the waiter who attended us came with three other waiters with a very delicious looking chocolate cake. They approached our table and asked my parents, "How long have you been married?", to which mom replied "Thirteen years." And somehow everyone in a ten feet vicinity from us heard her say this, and as fellow Chicagoans they started to clap towards my parent like if they won an Oscar. Being a little six-year-old, I hated all the attention and I wanted to hide. The clapping lasted a little over ten seconds before everyone returned to eating. My parents finished their chocolate cake while I asked the waiter for three boxes for takeout. We put the pizza in the boxes and left.

Chicago is perceived as this war infested place, where violence and anarchy are common, but Chicago is filled with family-friendly places, like Connie's, scattered all around the city. All you need to do is come and see for yourself.

Daniel R. is a fourteen-year old who attends Jovita Idar Academy. Daniel has lived in Chicago for all of his life, and would one day like to move to California like all the "Big Dreamers". He lives with both his parents, his sister, grandmother, and his dog. Daniel is a genius when it comes to video game logic and facts, and he's also very interested in robotics, aerospace, and aerodynamics (he's an ultimate nerd). In his free time, he likes to play video games, code, and brainstorm ideas for robots. Nothing is stopping him from succeeding in life.

CHOICE

BY JESUS C.

My Chicago is
a place of diversity.
Living
where all around us, death's existing.
A place where the bold face the timid.
A place where you can either
face your fears or you can drown in them.
A city where town meets skyscrapers, meets water, meets waves, meets
the surfers.
Where seasons meet and sicknesses breathe.
My Chicago is also a place where young minds feed.
Where youth blossoms and limitations are deceased.
Your fear is your fire.
In this cold world, you gotta stay hot. In the windy city, be consumed
or shine bright.
So light the way, 'cause Chicago says
everyone has a dream.
And family's
the tortilla that's holding together the meat.
Some work with it, some won't.
Ride the Loop, you may experience,
you can witness,
some don't give a fuck. Some really believe in giving care.
Some will share,
some are greedy.
Either way, it gives us hope.
My Chicago tells you to be whomever you seek.
A diamond, birthed from immense pressure
Beauty is found
in the dark,
living bright.
Illustrating visions that are so astounding.

My city is a large diverse one, still a part of our country, and a part of our world.

Fundamentally, we will find love, we will find fear. In the city that bares such, I've learned from.

We all have a choice, and a path to follow, you choose.

Jesus Enrique C. is an unorthodox paradox whose balance is of significance. According to Jesus, his love is his shield, and his knowledge is his weapon. At eighteen years old, he has already lived in many different places among all types of people, and as a result he can adapt to any social situation like a chameleon. He lives by the motto, "We're an expression of the universe itself."

FOR THE LOVE
OF CHICAGO
AND MY FAMILY

BY MELANIE C.

Before 2012, my family moved around a lot. I don't remember too much about the cities I lived in. I remember my siblings being born and my family growing, but nothing stood out to me about any of the places we moved. All that mattered was that my family grew and that we were together. Then, in 2012, I moved to Chicago, and my city became home to me and my family.

When I first laid my eyes on Chicago I couldn't remember a single thing about it. How did I feel? Well, I was just shy and uncomfortable because when I met my aunts and uncles and cousins I felt like they were complete strangers; I never had the confidence to talk to anyone before because we moved around so much. I never really had the chance to get to know people well enough, even my own relatives! Chicago helped change all that. I was finally somewhere where we took the time to get to know each other and I do love them more than ever! I have finally come out of my shell. Time has passed and so did our love - a great big family with my aunts and uncles and cousins.

I mean, we family members fight a lot and we all struggle with so many challenges, like kids being spoiled just to make our parents lives so miserable and humiliating. But that doesn't bother me because I get used to it. Like for instance, if we go to some neighbors house because of their birthday or a celebration, there would be some drama going on for like five minutes or less. If that ever happens I would ask my mom or dad for their phone and watch Youtube or play some games that they downloaded or I would just sleep while the drama goes on. But I love my memories, my friends, and anything that makes me feel compassionate and honest about the way I truly am.

And I will always love Chicago and my family. They are precious to me. Chicago is my home and that's where I want to be always and forever. No matter what, Chicago will always truly be where I am from. Chicago is where I first became a sister to a sister. Chicago had moments that were full of emotions and things that happened that are very special to me and my family. Like for instance, that time where we went to visit my mom's sister that she hadn't met for a long time and when my mom and her sister met in person they were happy and I was happy for them.

Melanie C. is a fourteen-year-old girl who is Mexican and loves comedy shows and reading manga (Japanese graphic novels). Her favorite activity to do during after school is drawing stuff that pops out of her mind (yet she is terrible at drawing but doesn't care). She loves to eat different kinds of foods like maybe chocolate, tangerines, or chips that are in her house. She isn't a fan of listening to any lectures but listens to them so she can improve her grades and likes trying out new food she's never tried before, but she doesn't like raisins.

STORY OF
MY LOVE LIFE

BY JAMAL W.

I found love in Chicago at Michele Clark High School, but we had been talking before that. April 8th, 2017 - I found the LOVE OF MY LIFE. I was still in 8th grade while she was a freshman. We met through a mutual friend of ours. At first we was just talking, not too serious, but then something I can't explain happened. When we first seen each other was at my cousin's party in April, that following week we met. When we first seen each other I was happy and nervous 'cause I was already excited from the party. After that night we was talking ever since. In the summer we was on and off even though we were young. I chose to go to the same high school as her so we could be together everyday. Now we are ten months as of a week ago. April 8th, 2018 we will be one year. WOW!!! We love each other deeply and this relates to Chicago because Chicago has so many romantic sites to find love in for dates. We went to Navy Pier Winter WonderFest and we got on all the rides and ate a funnel cake - IT WAS FUN! I LOVE MY GIRLFRIEND.

The reason I love her is because she's always here for me and she always supports me through anything. This girl is always here for me through the ups and downs. An up we had was when she was there for me when I love her with all my heart. Good or bad, mad or sad, she's here. My family loves her, her family loves me, and that gives me hope we're going to last long. We have arguments everyday but we get through them like any normal couple would. We never knew from the first time we started talking that we would last long but we're here now. I found her and I'm not letting her go. We joke, we laugh, we play, we can never go without each other. I'm so protective over her, I wouldn't let nobody do anything to her.

I can't wait 'til we make a year, that will be the happiest time of my life because we're so young and that's a long time to be with someone at this age. She's met my parents and I've met hers, and our families love each other as we got to know each other over the months. Her mom calls me her son because she says she never met a boy that treated her daughter so good and that's respectful. My mother and sisters love my girlfriend because they see that she makes me happy and they see she's very respectful and understand that I had other females in my life before her. My older brother even took us on our first date and our first date went very well. We went to Buffalo Wild Wings, and we had hot wings and nachos, and after we went to the mall and I bought her something from Pink. We went to my house after and I gave her her last gifts which were a ring, perfume, and earrings. It went very well and she was so happy with what I bought. That moment was everything and very special to me. We've grown stronger over the past couple of months and I'm grateful for the moments we share. I'm happy she's in my life because without her in my life, life would be boring. I appreciate the time she put in me to make me a better person because before I met her I was always outside in the Austin community and doing bad stuff with my friends. I didn't use to care about nothing, I used to be a troubled child to the Austin community. Always outside, messing with people, doing illegal things, just being a trouble kid. But then she came along and changed me for the better and I'm grateful she did because if she hadn't done that, there's no telling where I would be and what I would have been doing without her occupying my life and time. She came into my life and made me a better person. That's why I love her and will always will love her - she made me a better person.

Jamal W. is fourteen years old and attends Michele Clark Magnet School. He is a ninth grader. He was born and raised in Chicago. He enjoys technology such as his phone, his video game, and television. He is very spoiled because he is the youngest of five children. He loves eating junk food and riding his hoverboard. He loves listening to music and doesn't like school very much. He's very energetic and active. In his free time, he enjoys doing fun activities such as zip-lining, going to Skyzone, and going to Six Flags. He also loves eating hot fries.

THE BEAUTY OF CHICAGO

BY ROBERTO S.

It was nighttime, the moon was bright like the sun, and it was windy like other usual days. It was different this time because my grandma had never been in downtown Chicago before. So we were going to places around downtown, even some places that I'd never been to. Our first stop was the lakeside view. When we got there it was beautiful, every single thing was beautiful, nothing was terrible. The lake was dark blue. It looked pleasing.

The most beautiful thing out of this point of view were the skyscrapers. Each one was brightly lit and each one had different colors. It was like a light festival going on in the skyscrapers. There was one skyscraper that stood out of all of them. It was the Willis Tower. It was tall and bright. It's a unique skyscraper, very different from all the other buildings in Chicago. That's why it's such a special building and an icon of Chicago. All the beauty of Chicago amazed me. I couldn't believe what I was seeing. I was surprised as much as my grandma was. This was her first time seeing Chicago and I was here for all of my life, and I've never noticed how beautiful Chicago was. This moment changed my whole point of view of Chicago in many ways. This moment gave me a lot of pride of being raised in Chicago, and not to be afraid to show it. This also showed me that Chicago is not all about all the violence and crime that's going on here. That's just a small picture of Chicago. Many people only know that small picture of Chicago, which disappoints me that they only know that picture. This view will prove anyone that believes that Chicago is unsafe and it's always a warzone in here that all of that is just a small picture. You should know the full picture.

Some hours later from the last place we went to, we decided to go to downtown to see the Christmas tree be turned on. I hadn't seen the Christmas tree turned on in a long time, so I was excited to see it happen again. There were a lot of people around the tree like if a parade is going on here. I could tell that everyone was excited to see this happen. People started to do the countdown, "5, 4, 3, 2, 1!" and when the tree lit up, so did all the people's faces. The tree was tall and colorful.

It looked delightful. Everybody started to get excited like it was New Year's. When I saw all the people getting excited I felt some happiness and pride going through me. This is how the real Chicago is. This was one of the most wonderful moments I've experienced in Chicago. My grandma was surprised by all the lights of the tree and the beauty, but I wasn't surprised. I've experienced more beautiful things in Chicago, but this memory makes the Chicago that I know and love.

Roberto S. is a fourteen-year-old. He's an eighth grader in Jovita Idar. He's lived in Chicago for most of his life. He has one brother, one sister, and a dog and don't forget about his parents! He wastes most of his life playing video games and doing homework. He also loves eating food (who doesn't?).

OASIS OF HOME

BY MIRANDA R.

While my sister is unpacking,
I take off my sandals
and feel the hot sand against my feet.
It hurts but I endure it
until my feet are comfortable in the sand.
Whenever I take a step,
I feel the soft sand against my feet.

I walk to the water
and when the shores comes up,
I feel the cold water of Lake Michigan splashing under me.
Relieving all of the stereotypes and the violence that Chicago has.
I walk closer to the water when it reaches
all the way up to my knees. I look down and see
these tiny little shells,
thinking if I pick them up they would break.

I look around seeing people playing,
relaxing, and laughing.
Realizing that this is
our Oasis of Home.

Miranda R. is an eighth grader that has lived in Chicago for almost all of her life. Miranda's favorite thing to do is to stay inside her home and spend time on her tablet or on her phone. What she dislikes is going outside, school, and her dad telling her to take off her headphones. Miranda dreams of being an artist and showing her artwork. She is always inspired by a lot of anime art and cartoons. She hopes that she can complete that dream and work hard for that dream to come true.

IF THE BUS
COULD SPEAK

BY JAYLIN F.

5:00 a.m. I wake up, take a shower in five minutes, run a pick through my hair, and put on my clothes. 5:56 a.m. I leave the house, take the two minute walk to the bus stop. The street lights are still on, their bright orange color dispersing the dark. It has been raining all night. The light's reflection is crisp, and it is only obstructed by the small craters in the road. It's a little chilly. The bus arrives. I enjoy seeing fluorescent lights pierce through the darkness, drawing my concentration straight to the windows. The bus is quiet. I walk to the back and take a seat. There are a few people riding the bus, but I pay no attention to them.

The ride to the Red Line doesn't take too long from Bennett. I get off and cross the street in front of the bus. I look down while crossing, watching for the green light reflecting off the street from the traffic sign, but all of my focus is on the red of the stoplight reflected from the wet asphalt. I reach the train station and walk down the stairs. I pass through the gate where the darkness and fluorescent lights await. I walk through the door past two sets of seats and wait. This part is my favorite: the silence, the isolation in public places, the calm. Cars running on the highway create a white noise that engulfs me. I pull out my phone and headphones and put each earbud in place, plug the jack into the phone, and play "Everyday," by A$AP Rocky. This day, taking public transportation is beautiful, but public transportation can have its asinine moments too.

January 24, 2018. I left school and headed over to the bus after finally realizing there was one coming. After staring off into space for a while, I crossed the street, then headed for the bus stop. A few moments later, a man walked up to me. The man was Caucasian and wore dreads, two white earrings, and a black jacket.

"This bus is going to the Red Line?" he asked.

"Yes," I replied.

He walked away and started talking to a man behind me. The bus arrived shortly after that. I walked to the back and sat on the right side of the bus. A few moments after sitting down, the man came to the back. There was another man already in the back of the bus to my left; he was

African-American. The man who came to the back started talking to the man on the other side of me. I paid no mind to what they were talking about. Almost instantly, the man sitting next to me said, "no," in a polite but very dismissive way.

At the next stop, several people got on. A man and woman came to the back. The man was African-American, and he was wearing a durag, a black jacket and black jeans. The woman wore a large puffy tan coat, and she was also African-American; they sat across from each other. After everyone sat down, the bus started moving. The man with dreads started talking to the man in the durag who had just sat down.

"What did you just ask me?" the main with the durag said.

"I asked you if you had any crack," the man with dreads replied.

Even though I had heard what they said, I decided not to make eye contact with either of them because I didn't want to be dragged into anything.

"Why would you ask me something like that!?" The man with the durag was genuinely pissed. "That is not okay. Even if I did have some, I wouldn't give it to you!"

The ride went on like this for a while, with the woman occasionally chiming in to say that there are certain ways to ask a person this kind of question, and every black person doesn't do the same thing. When we got to Western, the man in the durag asked the man with dreads why he had asked him out of all the people on the bus.

"My friend told me to look for a certain type of person that looked like you," the man with the dreads said.

In response, the man with the durag's face changed, taking on a look of shock mixed with anger--signifying that the man with the dreads should take back what he just said. Almost immediately, the man wearing dreads started to apologize for jumping to conclusions. The African-American man started to cool down. The majority of the bus ride went on in this way. Things seemed to be fine. The man was still ranting, but not as loudly. Meanwhile, the rest of the bus was avoiding the conflict in the back of the bus altogether. A few moments later, the man with the durag seem to get irritated that this had actually happened to him.

"So if I did have crack, why would I give it to you?" the man with the durag asked.

"Do you have some?" the man with the dreads asked.

The tension in the air returned, but this time it was only focused in one person. The man with the durag's face was no longer calm, it was enraged. You could tell everyone on the bus was getting very uncomfortable, you could tell by how quiet it was on the bus, and everyone knew how the plot could unfold.

"Where are you getting off at?" the man with the durag said.

"At the Red Line," the man with the dreads replied.

We were on Halsted, so it would take no time at all for the bus to get there.

"You got some money?" the man with the durag asked. The tone of his voice was hoarse and no longer sounded as light and forgiving as it once did.

"No," he replied.

"How are you going to ask somebody for something when you don't even have the money to pay for it?" the main with the durag asked. "You have a card."

"Ya, why?" the man with the dreads asked.

"Because it just so happens I'm getting off at the Red Line too."

I glanced around and saw the man sitting on the other side of me looking out the window, shaking his head. The man with dreads looked worried, as if he had just caught onto what was going on.

He started looking around.

"What are you looking around for?" the man with the durag asked. "This is between you and me, and if any anything were to happen, they would be on my side. If I were you, I'd get off the bus right now. What do you think I'm going to do once we get to the Red Line?"

The bus was on Lafayette, only a three-minute walk from the Red

Line, and the bus kept inching closer and closer. All of a sudden, the man with the durag's phone dinged. He looks at it.

"You've been saved by the bell," he said, looking directly at the man with the dreads. "Then again, maybe not. Tell you what: If you let me slap you one good time, I'll let this all go."

The bus arrived at the Red Line. The majority of the people got off the bus, but right before the man with the durag got off, he grabbed the other man's dreads.

"You're harassing me," the man said matter-of-factly.

The man with the durag started quickly moving his hand around, dragging the other man's head every which way, but as quickly as it started, it was over. He let go and bent down to say something to the man with the dreads. The man with the durag proceeded off the bus and stared the man with the dreads down through the window of the bus.

New people got on the bus, with only a few privy to what had just transpired. The man with the dreads stayed seated. Some of the new arrivals came to the back, including an old man, a young man and a few others.

"Does this bus go another way on the Red Line?" the man with the dreads asked.

"No," I tried to say it in a comforting way, but I'm not sure if I succeeded.

The young man who had just sat down at the back of the bus handed him a bus card.

"It has one ride left," he said.

The man with the dreads got off at S Michigan Ave, and started walking back to the Red Line.

CTA has always been my major resource for transportation, and it has inadvertently also supplied me with many real world experiences that I'd never think could happen. From the drunk homeless lady taking a nap on my shoulder and occasionally waking up to curse people who said she smelled to the old man with a knife trying to fight a lady, Chicago's public transportation has supplied with me with countless experiences that I probably can't--and hopefully won't--get anywhere else. In conclusion, it's probably safer to just get a car.

Jaylin Le'Antwoine F. is seventeen years old and was born in Chicago. He moved to Carbondale, IL at the age of two with his father, mother and brother. At the age of seven, he moved back to Chicago with his sister and soon-to-be stepfather. A year later, in 2009, his sister passed. Fast forward to November 2015, he got sick and stopped going to school because of his illness for about a year. Jaylin then enrolled at Pathways in Education.

THE
HEAVENLY SIDE

BY IVAN M.

One summer day, my dad asked my brothers and me if we wanted to go ride our bikes. Obviously we said yes, so we grabbed our water and our bikes and left as soon as my dad finished eating. After we finished eating, we put our bikes on the bike rack and got in the car. It was me, my mom, dad, and two little brothers who left and it took a long time. I thought we were never going to get there. Finally we were downtown and could not find any parking so I wanted to go home, but we got lucky and found a parking spot right in front. We were riding our bikes and the wind just felt so good that I did not want to stop. My dad took us by the lake and I saw everyone enjoying themselve and I don't know what I was trying to do, but it was some crazy things. I sat right in front of the lake and saw the sun set and that was really beautiful. Waves were splashing and the smell was awesome and I just wanted to get into the water but it was really cold.

Every good story has to come to an end. My ten year old brother saw me riding my dad's bike and thought he could ride it too. He had everything fine until he almost fell into the lake with my dad's bike and, if it wasn't for this random lady and my mom, he would have fallen in. Luckily there was no major injuries. I was scared that he almost fell but it was still pretty funny. We packed up our drinks and our food and sadly had to go home, but overall I had a great time. We got back to the car, got some Little Caesars pizza, and went home to chill and play video games.

I have never felt really free in my entire life, but I felt one with the air this day. I felt really relaxed but really tired. Other than playing soccer and video games, bikes is the next the best thing unless I am really worn out.

I learned that life isn't about using what you are comfortable with. It's about getting away from this modern day technology and exploring the world. Maybe a simple thing like going outside but you have to go outside and be adventurous. Don't be afraid to show your inner self. Show the people who you are on the inside where people can't see. Once in while, go outside. There is more in the world than just technology and your phone. I experienced this in Chicago with my family while we rode our bikes downtown. You don't have to like bikes, find something you love and do it outside. Read, play soccer, or pretty much anything else. Go explore Chicago and see our city, our beautiful city.

Ivan M. is an eighth grader who attends at Jovita Idar and has been living in Chicago ever since he was born. He loves to play soccer and pretty much plays everyday. Ivan is a freak for math and it's his favorite subject. Ivan watches gaming Youtube videos for fun. Ivan loves Chicago for his friends and family.

ONE PERFECT SUMMER

BY ADAJA C.

The 90 degree weather

The daily days and nights with my cousins.

Going to the carnival almost every week, going on the rides together. Linking up about almost everyday.

Going to the beach, walking around and exploring while we share chisme.

Going to Navy Pier, to take pictures with the skyscrapers and going on the rides there.

Going to the nearest paleteria for paletas de limon and just spending time together.

We hardly see each other so when we do we try and enjoy every moment we have together.

Sleepovers at each other's house every other day.

The places we go make those adventures in Chicago special to me.

As the days go by, the end of summer gets closer and closer.

The nights get longer and the days get shorter.

As the summer comes to an end we fade and eventually grow apart.

Days have passed and I haven't seen or spoken to them.

Although throughout the months we don't talk, the memories that remain in my heart and the places are what represent My Chicago.

Adaja C. is a fourteen year old Hispanic girl at Acero Idar. She was born and raised in Chicago. Adaja lives with four of her siblings and likes to be outgoing, wild, and adventurous (sometimes). But at the same time she is very quiet.

WRITING PROMPT 3:

Write 9 lines about the following topics. You can use the first line provided or make your own up.

A. WHY YOU LOVE CHICAGO-
Start with: Of the many reasons I love Chicago, here is one...

B. WHAT ANGERS YOU ABOUT CHICAGO-
Start with: The tension builds inside of me when...

C. WHAT'S THE FUTURE OF THIS CITY-
Start with: I stand here looking ahead...

MY CHICAGO WORLD

BY EVANGELINA M.

On a really windy and chilly day, I was on my way to Lincoln Park with my friends, talking and looking out the window around the city. All the people talking with their peers, the waves of the Chicago lake giving some type of chill mood. As we got to the park near the zoo we saw a couple of families with their kids. A couple of people walking around the city walking by the lake with a coffee in hand. Adults taking pictures of the city, sharing the good time they're having. Getting closer, I got excited to meet some more of my friends there.

Crossing the little bridge to get to the Lincoln Park Zoo, you could see people taking pictures there. Some use that view to take pictures of the city, the small river under us, a really nice landscape filled with small little flowers and trees with beautiful white flowers hanging from them. The warm sun was softly hitting our backs, but the wind was kind of cold. The theme going on in Chicago was pretty chill. As we entered the zoo we saw so many families with their kids. The smile on their faces, pointing at animals in excitement. Walking around with my friends, taking note of the animals, taking silly pictures in front of the animals, full of energy to keep going.

As we were playing truth or dare behind the food court of the zoo, we saw the face painting stand. One of my friend dared the other to get her face painted as a tiger. As we were heading towards the stand we were all laughing at her. We couldn't even believe that she was actually doing it. As she got her face painted as a tiger, we were behind her waiting for it to be finished. We were getting anxious every time the guy picked up the little sponge as he put it down and then dabbed some paint on it. Finally, as she turned around, we all burst out into laughter. She looked more like a weird mouse than a tiger. As we were walking out to just walk around downtown, her face was still painted like a tiger. Talking with friends, full of energy and still laughing a little. Even though we had most of the people looking at us, because she still had her face painted, we still had fun. Heading to buy some food, that delicious pepperoni pizza, not too much of something, or too little, the right amount for us. Walking all around town, looking at so many amazing places: The Crown Fountain, The Bean, taking pictures next to it, near it. Walking down Lake Michigan looking at the waves.

Heading back to the car to go back home, we passed by all these really nice murals. Some of the best street art I've ever seen. Some people might not like it because they think it's just a bunch of "art", but if they knew the history behind it, it's just amazing. All related to Chicago and how so many people started from here, full of the best opportunities. Even if there's a bunch of people talking bad about Chicago, and how "dangerous" this place is. Nobody really knows how great Chicago is but the people that have actually experienced it. We're anxious to get home. We're exhausted after so much walking. Taking a nap on the drive back home, finally getting there and being able to finally shower then rest after a long journey in downtown Chicago.

Through these trips that I've taken with either my family or friends, I've gotten closer with them. I learned a bunch of stuff and learned more about my parents and their lives before they came here. Chicago really has nice places to hang out with family, if it's either restaurants, cookouts in our backyard, or at the park after a soccer game. We enjoy hanging out with each other while listening to actual good music if it's corridos or rancheras. Chicago allows our family to express ourselves, for example our Mexican culture. Chicago is genuinely full of happy places. You should come and visit and find your own.

Evangelina M. is a fourteen-year-old, soon to be fifteen. She lives in Chicago. She enjoys anything to do with art. She loves it when it's summer, because she can go play soccer in the park with her brothers and cousins. Most of the people she knows call her "Shorty" because she's really short. She has three brothers that are really annoying but she still loves them all. She also loves both of her parents.

NOVEMBER

BY PAOLA S.

The wind is whistling around my short mousy hair,
making the strands that have fallen dance
in the same direction the wind blows.
Jimi Hendrix blasts through my headphones,
just neatly sitting in my ears.
My shoes are splashing in the half frozen puddles.
The air feels like needles stabbing my face,
but I ignore it.
Hot coffee melts down slowly to my stomach.
My hands are tightly gripping my jacket,
searching for at least a bit of warmth.
But I ignore it.
All I can actually think about is him.
The one I walk in 10-degree weather for.
The one who shows me around my city,
Like if the city just rose in a blink of an eye.
Like an undiscovered forest,
yearning for adventure.
Like a child experiencing light for the first time.
Excitement and curiosity rushes through my veins,
like the ocean swallowing a small pebble by the shore,
completely and entirely.
That's exactly how I was pulled in.
He looks like the last beautiful rose that blooms,
right before the cold weather arrives.
I find him patiently sitting on the Marquette Park bench,
by the garden.
This is where I found love in this loud,
reckless,
noisy,
but fascinating city of Chicago.

Paola Ruby S. is seventeen years old and was born in Chicago. She moved to the suburbs at nine years old and moved back to the city at seventeen. She loves makeup and loves the outdoors. She loves metal, rock, and alternative music. Her dream is to become a tattoo artist.

A CITY THAT
STANDS UP
FOR ITSELF

BY RICHARD A.

We had gotten off the mustard yellow school bus and now had been waiting under the building pavilion for about twenty minutes while the rain slowly turned into a light mist. The first thing I saw was people shouting and yelling for change. I felt proud that in my city, people don't wait for politicians to make changes, they tell them to do it now. A whole cacophony of sounds hummed in the air, ranging from a trumpet to a vihuela. But that was nothing compared to the roar of people gathered there at the protest.

We had come to play at the protest in front of the Thompson Center, a round, red building covered in reflective windows. Even though it had been drizzling, the people protesting in front of the federal building hadn't backed down and were sticking to their goal. We were just a beginning mariachi at that time and only knew two songs, "El Rey" and "La Bamba".

At last the raindrops had dissipated enough to be able to not to get much more than a few drops of rain on you while not being under the protection of the building's pavilion. Walking up the stairs to the stage you couldn't help but feel the water from the rain underfoot. There were still raindrops on the stage and microphones, gleaming in the weak sunlight of the cloudy afternoon. The people were gathered here to protest about the injustice of not giving enough funds to schools. I was in one of those schools.

Standing up there on the stage I could see the multitude of people joining together to fight for what is right. You could see the sweat glistening on the faces of the people taking part in the protest, riled up to demand justice and more funds for schools. As soon as we got our instruments into playing position the crowd soon got quiet. Our music teacher gave the count and we burst into a song. While playing I could see the excitement on the faces of our audience. There was an African-American woman saying, "Whoo, I love this music!" She didn't even know what the lyrics were or what the song was about. She was so open-minded that she accepted it without a thought. Just like how many people in our city are like, diverse and open-minded. Able to accept others beliefs and cultures.

After we finished that song we played another one and when we were done, I felt almost bad about how we only played so little. They seemed to really enjoy it. We bowed then turned around, walking back down the slippery steps, some of us slipping a little. The buses that were supposed to pick us up weren't here yet so we had to wait for them under the pavilion. We got our instrument's cases and put them back inside. The DJ started the music up again. We had nothing else to do so we took pictures of our reflections in the windows.

As I was boarding the sunflower yellow school bus I realized the reason why they wanted us to play there was because we are people from Chicago that work together, from the youngest to the oldest. And it doesn't matter if you are Mexican, black, or whatever race you are. We don't care. We are a diverse city and it is in our interest to defend our rights as citizens, humans, and people as a whole too. We're great whether you care or not and we are going to keep it that way. When I was reflecting on this I noticed that outside the window of my seat I gazed at a black and white coral-like artistic statue that even still to this day I cannot fathom an idea to what it represents. Watching it fade away as the bus moved forward.

Richard A. (eighth grade) wrote this when he was fourteen and wants to go to Jones College Prep. He is waiting for a response from the school and it's going to probably come next month. He plays trumpet at the Mariachi Institute of Chicago (search it up on Facebook and give it a big thumbs up) and has played it since fourth or fifth grade (he says he can't remember correctly, he has a memory like that). He loves Chicago for all it's different food varieties and has lived here since day one.

"AND I'M FROM"

BY MARIAH E.

And I'm from the part of the city where everywhere you go you hear gangbanging.
Where people "merch" it on your name,
where there are the homeless out on every street,
where instead of helping the needy they just get greedy.

And I'm from the part of the city where people reported hearing shootings
and their mother cries knowing they're not safe but she tells her kids that anyway.

And I'm from the part of the city where jobs are hard to get
and when they give up they dine on a bottle of wine.
Where knowing that you want to succeed but the dreams are hard to meet.

And I'm from the part of the city where your parents tell you to look both ways as you walk
because their kids are getting kidnapped everyday on the streets as we talk.

And I'm from the part of the city where you get 9 o'clock curfews,
just knowing that you aren't going to follow the rules.

And I'm from the part of the city that's called: Chicago

Mariah E. attends Michele Clark High School. She is in the ninth grade and fifteen years old. Growing up she started off rough because she wasn't paying attention in school and was off track with what she needed to do. After the fifth grade, she started to be more excited about school and realized how school can make you have a successful future. After that, she started getting better grades and participating more in school. She got on the honor roll and was one of the top students in her class. She knows high school is just another step into getting to where you need to be in life. High school for Mariah started off good and it's still good because she's learning more and more things that she didn't know in elementary school.

THE
WONDERS
OF
CHICAGO

BY MARELYN M.

My Chicago is family.

The Riverwalk is full of my family memories.

My little brother's eyes are as blue as the water and his curious little face lights up as soon as he sees the boats stream down the river.

You don't know how wonderful Chicago is unless you have walked through the beautiful Millennium Park.

My Chicago is home.

I feel so much comfort.

There is just such a great sense of pride to be here.

I belong.

I feel honored to be here.

You don't know how beautiful Chicago is unless you have heard a true Chicagoan talk about their land.

So don't let the dark voices ruin your Chicago.

Open your eyes a little wider,

listen a little longer,

and discover the wonders of Chicago.

Marelyn M. is a fourteen-year-old Latina that is currently attending Jovita Idar (: She has lived in Chicago for the past twelve years. She is the oldest of three children. She is an ordinary girl with big dreams. She's on a long term mission to become a therapist and to help lots and lots of little kids with several disabilities.

MY CHICAGO

BY ASHLEY O.

When I was young, I always sought adventure. I was a mere eight or nine years old when I would ask my mom to take my younger sister Lety, and me downtown. I wanted to ride the train, walk around, and look at all the beautiful tall buildings that Chicago is known for. I grew tired of looking at our dingy, rundown neighborhood. We lived in Little Village at the time, which was known for the heinous shootings and abandoned buildings that no one lived in for years where teenagers would go to do drugs and drink. I wasn't even ten yet and I knew all of this already.

I wanted to do something new, something exciting for once. I wanted to get out of the only neighborhood that I knew and just escape for a while. My mom worked a nine-to-five Monday through Friday, so for the most of the summer Lety and I were in the care of our older cousin, Linda. She tried making our summer fun for the most part. She would take us to the park and to the mall. She even bought us a small pool that we could enjoy on the hot summer days. After a while, we became bored of doing the same thing over and over again. We wanted to do something new, and I think she was starting to notice. One of those days when she was serving us breakfast, she asked us what we wanted to do. My eyes instantly lit up. I knew exactly what I wanted to do. Without hesitation I blurted out, "Let's go downtown!" She smiled.

"That's a great idea. I'll talk to your mom and we'll see if we could go tomorrow."

I could not contain my excitement. I could feel my heart beating through my chest. That only lasted a second though. What if my mom says no? I thought to myself. She has to say yes, right? These questions raced through my mind and I became anxious as the time that my mom got home approached. After what seemed like days, my mom finally got home. As she entered through our front door, we ran up to her excitedly, asking her about the plans that we had made for the next day. And she said yes! I was so happy and excited, even more than I had been earlier that day when I had first asked Linda about going downtown.

The following day, Lety and I woke up bright and early with my mom and prepared our outfits to wear that day. Like most days when we went out, my mom chose matching outfits for us. I usually hated it, but that day I wasn't going to wait. As soon as Linda got there, we wanted to leave right away, but we couldn't. We had to have breakfast, shower, and get ready. After all that was done, we got to finally leave!

We took the train downtown. I sat by a window seat and just stared out of it. I was fascinated and thought to myself, How are we going so fast without falling off the tracks? But I quickly made myself diminish the thought because it scared me. Staring out the window made me realize how big Chicago really was and how I had only seen a small portion of it my whole life. The ride seemed too fast. When we got to our stop, I didn't want to get off - I wanted to see more. We got off on a busy street and didn't even take ten steps when I stopped in my tracks to stare at all the beautiful tall buildings, all the people pacing down the crowded street, and the cars that seemed to be stuck in rush hour. That didn't make sense to me because it was only about eleven in the morning. We walked a few blocks until we reached Millennium Park. The whole walk there we were silent, clearly starstruck by everything we had never seen before. There were a whole bunch of little shops everywhere that sold different things; there were sandwich shops, ice cream shops, fancy little restaurants. The combination of all the sweet and salty smells was so invigorating. I had never been in love, but I think this day that's all I felt.

When we finally approached the park, we were ecstatic to see the giant mirrored Bean that appeared to be even larger than our apartment building back home. There were also two giant pillars that had people's faces on them and seemed to be spewing out water. Everything was so awesome and I was ecstatic. The whole day had been filled with adventures. By the end of the day, I couldn't wait to get back home to our "dingy run down neighborhood" that throughout the day I grew to love. I realized how amazing and beautiful my city was and that our neighborhood was a part of it. I couldn't have been any more proud to be from Chicago that day.

Ashley O. is nineteen years old. Born and raised in Chicago's Little Village neighborhood, she moved to the Chicago Lawn neighborhood when she was thirteen. She loves to read and listen to music during her free time. Her favorite sport is baseball and she loves the White Sox. She enjoys Chicago's warm sunny days and even the cold winter nights. She is excited to go to college after graduating and find a career that she enjoys. She looks up to her mother for being so hardworking and loving and and to her grandfather who was respected and loved by everyone and was also her father figure for most of her teenage years. She hopes to one day make them proud.

THE
HEIGHT
OF LIFE

BY RAUL L.

When I was eight years old, my family took me and my sister to Navy Pier. The first thing I saw at the pier was the Ferris wheel and how far high up it went. Me seeing that as an eight-year-old kid was like seeing the stairway to God in a big wheel form. But sadly we were not going to the Ferris wheel first, so me and my family went around the pier looking at all the little things here and there. 4:30 p.m.

I went into the kids museum. Seeing science as a young kid was like watching a magic show but without the magic. Seeing this showed me that I could make anything and everything if I can put my mind to it. I had the best time messing around with all the little toys there. But as a kid you don't really care about all of that anyway. At least I had some fun messing around with what they got. 6:45 p.m.

When me and my family are going to eat, most of the time I'll just stuff my face on whatever. But when I took a bite of a hamburger that my mom gave me, that was the best thing I ever tasted in my short life. Like someone put a bomb of flavor in my mouth. I wanted to eat slowly to fully experience the taste of that burger. I was the last person to finish eating my food. 7:26 p.m.

It was time to go on the rides, but the only ride I wanted to go on was the Ferris wheel. I just wanted to feel like I was flying on an iron bird, but with a lot more safety on the bird. No one wanted to go with me so I went alone. I didn't mind at the time but now I wished I had someone else to share the experience. I forgot I was scared of heights. But now the wheel was turning and I had to sit down or start a waterfall of salty tears. Good thing I chose to sit down 'cause the next thing I needed then was an eight-year-old kid crying by himself in a Ferris wheel. 7:55 p.m.

I was at the top of the Ferris wheel. It was also growing dark so this would be the first and last ride that I'd ride that day. I was looking down in the little cart of the Ferris wheel most of the time because I was horrified looking down. But then I looked across and I saw the city lit up with all kinds of light: blue, green, yellow, purple. The whole city lit up like a Christmas tree in a dark room. The air was cool and soon after that

I got over my fear of heights and that is when I knew this was my home, my calling, my Chicago. 8:00 p.m.

Raul L. is a thirteen-year-old kid who lives in Chicago. He has a loving family with a pet dog named Fedo. His favorite song is "It's All Over But The Crying" by The Ink Spots. His superpower will be telekinesis. Most mornings he just wants to sleep for hours and hours.

A TRIP TO WINTER WONDERFEST

BY SHANIYA M.

On December 27th, my mother, sister, little cousin and I went to Navy Pier to have some fun at Winter Wonderfest. The trip was to celebrate Christmas and just do fun things you would do in the winter. They had indoor sledding, a lot of jumping houses, styled Christmas trees, food, hot chocolate, and more. When I first walked in, there was a giant Christmas tree about taller than a normal tree outside. The first thing I did was get on this Merry-Go-Round ride. It was so fun and it made me dizzy. After that we went to a food station because we were hungry. We ate tacos and donuts. At this point we had to let the food digest so we was just taking pictures and stuff until we were able to play and get on rides again. I really had a nice time. It was a very cool experience and if I could go again, I would. The best part to me was when we did indoor ice skating. This was fun to me because instead of being cold doing outside skating we can just enjoy the outdoors activities inside. They even had hot chocolate waiting for us after we were done skating. My mom bought all of us some.

Shaniya M. is a freshman in Chicago who attends Michele Clark High School. She enjoys shopping and hanging with friends. Fashion is something she is very interested in. She loves putting outfits together for people for special occasions when they don't know what to wear. She also loves babies and small children. When Shaniya grows up she wants to be a pediatrician and also continue her fashion career by starting her own clothing line.

CHICAGO'S
BEAUTIFUL FIELD

BY OSCAR M.

Chicago, home to many people,
places that are very cool to visit.
One place is Soldier Field.
You can feel the intensity of the crowd.
See the skyline to see the field,
the really beautiful field.

You can feel and see how amazing it is.
When you touch the grass, memories get in your head.
The field is beautiful,
it's not home to any team.
That doesn't mean no one can play there.

You can see how big and tall it is.
A pitch is more than a field,
it's where you want to be in the future.
This stadium is in the beautiful city of Chicago.

Oscar M. is a fourteen-year-old that has lived in Chicago his whole life. He's currently in Jovita Idar Academy. One of his favorite things is playing sports and hanging out with his friends. His favorite book series is *The Chronicles of Prydain.*

BASEBALL PRIDE

BY MANUEL D. L. R.

Chicago sports is a huge thing for me. It means a lot to me. One of the best memories that I have in Chicago is of baseball. When I was a kid I was watching baseball, and every time the Sox scored I'd be the happiest kid on earth. But when the other team scored, that would ruin my mood. Till this day I'm still a loyal White Sox fan. I may have other favorite teams but the White Sox are still my favorite.

Going to the White Sox Field is one of the best feelings you could have. It's like my second home. The smell of the food, hearing the crack of bat, hearing the ball hit the glove, the fireworks going off every time there's a home run, the people going crazy, and the smell of the grass. It's extremely amazing walking to the stadium, smelling the restaurants, and seeing the art on the walls. Probably one of the best things about Chicago. The best thing that has happened to me is the teams in Chicago. I remember going to my first game. Even though they lost, they still had fireworks. What I learned in that game is that even though you lose in a game that means you shouldn't give up. You still have another chance to win or give it your best shot. Life is like a baseball game, you get three tries to redeem yourself or to get revenge.

My background of baseball is because of my dad. What my dad told me is that he read books and that's what taught my dad to play baseball. Then he grouped with the kids in the rancho and made their own team. What I really liked about that is that they played different ranchos to see what team is the best. He taught me how to play and I'm pretty good at the game but I want to be better than good. One of the memories I have is that every day as a kid I'd tell my dad to take me to the park so that we could go play baseball. Everyone in my family loves baseball, mom's side and dad's side. Probably one of the best memories is me and my two cousins playing for the same team. And the thing is, my family came to watch us play together. Knowing that my family had to do something but still managed to come to see the cousins play. I feel like if I go somewhere, like travel somewhere else, it doesn't feel like Chicago. The smell of the air reminds me Chicago. It's one of the best feelings. Chicago is probably one of the best cities out there. Six months without baseball is pain in the butt. But now I'm back in training ready to hit dingers, to field every ball, and get better at baseball. I got to be honest, probably the best thing is laughing with my teammates, getting in trouble with the team, and running with my team. The field I play in is the biggest one. The farthest is 360ft to make home runs. But at the end of the day, my teammates are like my brothers to me.

There is nothing that can ruin that bond.

Manuel D. L. R. is a Fortnite pro. He has lived in Chicago for his entire life. He went to school at Jovita Idar. He plays baseball. He's a big fan of the Chicago White Sox. He dreams of going to the major league.

IN THE CITY
OF CHICAGO

BY ANONYMOUS

In the city of Chicago,
graffiti marks the walls.
In the city of Chicago,
tags drip on bathroom stalls.
In the city of Chicago,
etch bath ghosts the windows.
In the city of Chicago,
known for where the wind blows.
In the city of Chicago,
it's a Do-or-Die mentality.
In the city of Chicago,
rustoleum paints my reality.

CHRISTMAS IN CHICAGO

BY KEVIN L.

Some people think that Chicago is a place that has out of control gun violence and some website calls it one of the most dangerous places in the USA. But other people that don't live in Chicago only look at the violences and the death, not the good side of Chicago or, what I like to call "Windy City Christmas in Chicago." It's like a dream or like the movies that you see on TV. All the people are happy and there's people that sing songs that are so catchy like "All I Want For Christmas Is You." And when people are walking by the store you can hear the songs and all the people and you can feel the Christmas spirit. When you start to walk you can see the most beautiful and majestic tree in the world.

I remember the first day I went downtown to see the tree for the first time. It was like a dream came to life. It felt like looking at the stars and being hypnotized by how big and shiny it is. I was six and every year since that day, we have a tradition and we have do it. We get on the train at 7:00 p.m. and we get there at 7:45 p.m. then get some Chicago style coffee and some cookies. We just walk and look at the Christmas sales and we buy some Christmas ornaments or, what my mom says: "cute Christmas things." That day was the best. It was like going to the zoo as a child and looking at the animals and being amazed by the beautiful animals. That's how Chicago in winter and Christmas and beautiful places are because of the snow and the lights. It is the most beautiful. I can't explain, my mind tries to think of a perfect word but I don't have one. I have hundreds. It is one of those things that you cannot explain but you know it is wonderful.

And all the lights on the tree are like stars fallen from heaven and all the ornaments and the glitter on the things are like disco balls. People all over Chicago go to see the tree and when the families are taking picture they say they will never forget it. People get cold so they go to the vendors and go and get hot cocoa or coffee and Christmas themed food. And then I start to hear Christmas Carols and I remember that it's 10:45. My mom and dad say to me that we have go so then I say, "No." Then my mom says, "If we stay it can get crazy because of all the people moving." Then I say "No," again with a firm voice. She says "Okay," and looks at my dad. He looks at me like this kid is crazy and after all, it's after 10:00, so we stay on 'til it became Christmas then we left. When we get home my brother asks us, "How was the night?" and we say "Good." So then he says "Do you want to open the gifts?" we say "Yes." As soon as we open them my mom says "You can play with your toys tomorrow." And so that is how my day in Chicago and the good side that some people do not see in Chicago went. That's why I love my Windy City. Now do you see that on Christmas we all get together? It's not even the city, it's just the people in it.

Kevin L. has lived in Chicago for as long as he can remember. He goes to the school Jovita Idar. His favorite thing to do is dance and party with family and play volleyball on the warm summer days. Kevin will put himself over anyone else when he is older and goes to college. He wants to be a lawyer and fight for the people that cannot fight for themselves and to live in the city for as long as he can.

MY CHICAGO IS

BY TONY R.

A nice quiet city where you can sit outside
and enjoy the wind blowing through the trees and the leaves.
A place where people can be themselves
and not have to worry about people
not liking them for who they are.
A place where people can find some kind of inspiration.
A place where you can find weird but cool abstract sculptures
like the giant silver Bean and the tire sculpture in Millennium Park.
A dangerous place, but that doesn't mean you can't have fun in the city.
A place that is home to the Damen Silos,
the Navy Pier boat cruises to the middle of Lake Michigan,
and bipolar weather.

Tony R. is eighteen years old and moved from Little Village to Gage Park when he was about seven. He loves to play war games and explore abandoned and dangerous places. He dreams of joining the United States Marine Corps after graduating high school.

MARIACHI PRIDE

BY ALDO G.

I was backstage warming up and waiting for our cue. Mixed emotions ran through my body knowing there was going to be thousands of eyes watching me as I climbed on stage. The only reason I was here was because of the school mariachi participating and being directed by our music teacher Mr. Ozuna. We got our cue and we walked along these long hallways leading up to stage. As we climbed up, thousands of roars and claps emerged.

We began to take our spots and waited for Mr. Ozuna's count. Once he counted down to one, the music began to play. The music empowered the park with its enormous speakers playing the loud music. The adrenaline was rushing through my body as I told myself to relax and continue to play. As I played and watched the crowd, I saw thousands of people with smiles and cheer on their faces. They were watching the younger generation embracing their Mexican roots and letting them live by expressing it with music. Seeing all these people smiling and having this adrenaline made me realize that I would want to continue with mariachi. I was grateful that I had a teacher who gave me this opportunity that paved this journey of music that I wanted to pursue. I finished, took a bow, and walked off stage.

As we finished, the whole group went back to their seats and continued watching the show. As it got late at night, the park was still filled with thousands of people and the atmosphere reflected was amazing. There was an aroma of Mexican food and tacos flowing through the park. People lying on the grass, drinking margaritas and eating tacos, watching the mariachi play. It was a moment that just stuck with me, seeing the peace and love among us. And as I was in this Mexican Annual Chicago Festival, the Gay Pride Festival was happening at the same time throughout downtown. You might know this from Lady Gaga's historic mistake from the Instagram picture she took as she had mistaken the crowds. People with colorful flags flowed the streets of Chicago as you see gay people getting married throughout this.

This is the day that describes Chicago. The Chicago that is filled with diversity and love throughout its people. The randomness that happens in Chicago is just so common, us Chicagoans are used to it. Our Chicago unites together if we want to express our voices to the world. Multiple races with different cultures and beliefs coming together as one watching a show for pure entertainment as they are distracted from the world's troubles.

This was the first Millenium Park Mexican Festival in Chicago, one of the many parades and festivals that take place throughout this city. It is amazing how people look forward to the music and food parades that attract the millions of people across the nation.

Aldo G. is a fourteen-year-old eighth grader at Jovita Idar Academy. His dream is to attend Lane Tech High School and study computer science. He loves music and is part of one of the biggest student mariachis in Chicago. He enjoys Harry Potter books and loves working with technology. He hopes to become a computer engineer at Google Headquarters in California in the future.

I AM FROM
THAT PART
OF THE CITY

BY BRIANNA C.

I'm from the part of the city that they talk bad about
They say all our men is good at is
Gangbanging and selling drugs
And living their life as thugs
But it's not even like that
Where I'm from we fight back
They're mad at the fact that we are young, gifted, and black
I'm from the part of the city that they talk bad about
We are smart
Not just the words we say out of our mouths
We learn from our mistakes and
We walk by faith and not by sight
Maybe if everyone did that everything would go right

Brianna C. is a fifteen year old freshman who lives in Chicago,IL. She loves to sing, write songs, and rap. She enjoys to have fun with friends and family. Her favorite thing to do is to spend time with her mom and siblings. Brianna is a very intelligent and bright person. She has always had good grades in school by doing all of her work and staying on track. She loves to try new things but, does not try anything dealing with heights. Brianna is a different type of person. She loves to dress different from others and be the one in the spotlight.

THE
DOWNTOWN
EXPLORATION

BY LUIS M.

I am a child in Chicago and I want to tell you about my favorite places. One is the big Bean. I went there with my cousin and mom. After we went to The Bean, we went to the Sky Tower to look down and to see how beautiful the city looked. My mom did not want to go up in the tower because she is scared of high places. Once we were done looking at the city, my cousin and I went back to the first floor to be with my mom.

After we left the tower we went to Navy Pier. When we got to the pier we went shopping. When we left Navy Pier we went to go eat. I didn't get anything. Then we got back to the house and we slept together. I had a lot of fun at my favorite places in Chicago.

When we woke up, we decided to go downtown. We chose to go to the lake. I wanted to find out where the lake connects and if I could find any history behind the lake. I found out that the lake is connected to an ocean. That was confusing which made me think about the lake and what made it a lake that could turn into an ocean.

After we visited the lake it hit 12:45 so me and my family went to go eat at Navy Pier. We ate at Big City Chicken and I really liked it. The taste was so good I rated it a five out of five (in my head). After we ate we saw a popsicle stand and we all decided to get a banana dipped in chocolate with sprinkles. I liked how it was frozen and I also rated it a five out of five. Then we decided to leave and we went to go shop downtown.

When we finished shopping it was dark and me and my family headed to the park. At the park there was a firework show and me and my family decided to stay and watch the show. The show was so beautiful. It made me so happy to spend my time with the people that I loved the most. Around 9:00 p.m. we all decided to head back home. Home is something that I love and where I live in the neighborhood is calm. The neighborhood is fun, everyone shares what they have, and no one is greedy. This is truly a wonderful place to call home.

Luis M. is a thirteen year old kid that goes to Jovita Idar Academy. Luis lives in Chicago and his favorite hobby is soccer. He loves soccer because it is a lot of fun. His favorite spot in Chicago is the "big Bean" because you can see your reflection and there are always a lot of people looking at it. Luis lives with his mom, sister and brother. They are happy, but sometimes there are struggles they have to face. Luis has a pet chihuahua too. His dog is a boy named Canelo. Canelo wasn't in the family until they got him about two years ago. Someone found him in the street and then Canelo was given to Luis. Luis was amazed by the dog he was given. Luis loves dogs and was happy about caring for Canelo.

CHICAGO'S BEAUTIFUL SUMMER NIGHTS

BY LIZBETH M.

Strolling through Kostner in the late summer nights

Passing by the Midway airport, getting a taste of the colorful lights

Filling my face with joy

To look upon the night sky taking in the chill air

It couldn't get any better than to have my cousins to enjoy the moment with me

We all sit together and take a step back to deliberate

My cousins and I all talking pensively about what the future has in store for us

I feel so safe and content

We listen to calm, relaxing music that sets the vibe

As we are strolling through Kostner in the late summer nights

We've all had our memorable laughs

Unforgettable experiences

Everything we do is worth the risk for it brings delight to our adventure

Every night brings a new journey in our hands, and every night ending with a new incentive This all happens in one day, as we are strolling through Kostner in the late summer nights.

Lizbeth M. is fourteen years old, lives in Chicago, and loves Jesus Christ. She loves to be outgoing and physically active. Lizbeth loves to play soccer with her cousin. She is also a gamer that plays on her Xbox. Her family calls her Chaparrita because she is short. Lizbeth is a really goofy person and sometimes can't stay serious. When Lizbeth grows up she dreams to be an orthopedic surgeon.

CHICAGO THROUGH MY EYES

BY BRYAN O.

Many people say that Chicago has too much violence and that it's a bad place to live in. When seeing Chicago through my eyes, I see a pretty place that has many cool buildings. For example, The Willis Tower. Now that is one heck of a building! Let me just explain Chicago in my perspective.

Once, my brother and I went to the Blackhawks game (which they won!) and it was an amazing day! I would do anything to relive that day because they won the STANLEY CUP! The stadium got so crowded that some people kept jumping on top of other people. I kept getting anxiety when the other team kept catching up to the Blackhawks.

Anyways, let's stop talking about the Chicago Blackhawks and let's start talking about Chicago, also known as the Windy City. I love Chicago when its sunny because you can feel the sun's warmth caress your back and you can admire the great weather. Chicago has so many unique traits that I can't even name them all. But my Lord, when you see the skyline it looks AMAZING! You don't even want to take your eyes away from it. The skyline is just so mesmerizing to watch. It's home to the Willis Tower which is, in fact, the tallest building in Chicago. When it's night time, the tower looks so beautiful because it's the first one you see.

Chicago is a part of my life because I grew up here and it holds many of my memories. Chicago isn't only my home, it's home to many other places and people. For example, it's home to over 5,000 restaurants and also 56 museums. My favorite museum is the Shedd Aquarium and the crazy part is that I went there four years ago. Can you believe that Chicago has so many buildings? Oh, and here is another little fun fact: Did you know that Chicago is also called the "Working City", I mean I can tell by how many buildings we have!

What I'm trying to say is, Chicago is not a bad place. Yeah, we may have had a couple of crimes here and there but we aren't the only city who has crimes and violence. Every country and city has dealt with crimes so it's not just us after all. On a positive note, over 52 million people have visited Chicago annually and I bet that they enjoyed being here. Yeah, I know that Donald Trump has stated some bad things about Chicago but, Chicago has WAY more positivity than negativity. People are throwing shade at Chicago 'cause we are way better than they are. They just want to say bad things about Chicago when in reality it's a marvelous city. I am very grateful that I was born in CHICAGO!

Bryan O. is a thirteen year old who goes to a school named Jovita Idar Academy. He lives in a family of eight including his dog named Luigi. He is a big fan of the hockey team the Chicago Blackhawks. His hockey idol is Patrick Kane. Bryan has lived in Chicago since the day he was born and he has not gone to any other place. Bryan's hobbies include playing video games. His favorite game genre is horror. One of his favorite subjects is math.

THE GAME

BY ALEXIS Y.

It all started when my mom took me out of the private Christian Lutheran school. I was going into seventh grade. I was so glad to be getting out of St. Andrews. This was because I was constantly told I was going to hell because I did not believe the majority of what they were teaching. They would tell me that gays were going to hell, and that we should treat our bodies like temples. No tattoos, no smoking, and no drugs…Meanwhile, I have an uncle who is gay, I am bisexual, my father is a tattoo artist, and, at the time, my grandma smoked cigarettes. The school would say: "Everyone you're close to is going to end up in hell." I despised that school for the things they were trying to put in my head as a child. They told me that if I thought differently I was going to end up in hell too.

Flash forward to when I had started seventh grade. It was great. I loved being myself, I was able to make my own decisions on what religion I wanted to choose. I was happy until I needed to start applying for high school. I went to an Uno Charter school to finish grade school. They were super strict on how many high schools we applied to. They gave us a sheet of all the Nobel Schools. It showed schools like Lane Tech, Whitney M. Young, Walter Payton, Jones College Prep, Clemente, Robert Lindblom, and Chi-Arts. I applied to all and busted my ass to get all straight A's. I didn't get accepted into any of them. I was devastated, I was going to have to go to Kelly High School. I could not believe that I busted my ass to get nowhere.

I eventually fell into a depression. I didn't even want to go to my graduation. My life felt like it hit rock bottom. I was supposed to go to a good school to get a good start in life right? At this moment I was left in the dirt…until a couple days before graduation, my mom got a call from an unknown number. It was Chi-Arts! I was excited, overwhelmed, nervous, and so confused. They told my mom that I had to have four to eight finished pieces and then go in for an interview to see if I was eligible for the school. I was determined to finish the pieces in time! I didn't want to screw this opportunity up.

I was so anxious that I was not going to be good enough for the school since I had never even taken a class or read a book on drawing. I was just winging it at this point. I ended up drawing a rose, a woman in a Mardi Gras mask with feathers, a pair of lips, and lastly I took on a drawing of Audrey Hepburn that was only made up of dots. I was not really proud of any of the drawings I had done…but I had to try.

I went in for the interview and I was practically crapping my pants, but I did it. Two weeks later I got a call back and they wanted to do a follow up interview where they could really talk to me and ask me more in depth questions. They asked me questions like, "What type of dream job would you like do when you get older?" "What would you say your style of drawing is?" and "What is your interest in attending this school?" I was so overwhelmed and had a massive panic attack when I got into the car after the interview.

I eventually got a spot in Chi-Arts. I was so happy to be there. My teachers were super chill and taught me well. It was so different from what I was used to. I had conservatory homework for each class and academic homework for each class. The days were longer. I went from 8 a.m. to 5 p.m. non-stop working. I got used to the schedule eventually, but I had no time for anything. My home life was too much. I take care of my mom and help my dad out…I could not keep up with both at the same time. I was completely drained from all of the things I had to do. I fell back into a DEEP depression and was spiraling further and further down into a hole I could not get out of.

I let myself fail all of my classes and I would not got to school for months on end…I was having major panic attacks every time I would even go near the building. I felt like I was having a heart attack and I would get so tense I would pass out. I was eventually hospitalized for my depression and SI (suicidal ideations), but it didn't help. I was "fine" while I was in there, but nothing changed when I was released. I still didn't go to school and didn't care about anything…I still did not want to be here…or anywhere.

My father would tell me how the doctors couldn't help me. The only person who could bring me out of this was me. That's just what I did. I got myself out of the hole I was in. It didn't happen overnight, but I did it. I am now currently enrolled in Pathways in Education and I am getting my education one step at a time. I have learned from my worst times, and I am managing my life in Chicago based off of all my experiences.

Alexis (Lexi) Y. is a seventeen year old, who takes care of everyone around her. She has a passion for her art, and loves photography. Her dream job is to be an artist while dabbling in special effects cosmetology. Her personality is very caring and colorful.

BEHIND
BLOODY WALLS

BY HUGO P.

There is more to this city
Than the blood splattered barrier that is around us
There are colors that bring you to life
Faded dark shadows
Become colorful people
When lights turn on downtown

This is about a boy in Chicago
My broken heart felt alone
Because my "friends"didn't want to help
Even though I help them
I won't always be alone

My family took me into the city
To see the colors
Black and white begin
To fall away by bright light
To see the city
Makes me feel like I'm not caged in
I can do anything and nothing will hold me back
My loneliness will better soon
I used to sing "I'm not okay"
I used to say that I need help
The city colors bring me to confidence

 I see
So many people in love
Something I haven't felt yet
But I'm sure I will

Families and people with a big hearts
Not what you hear, humans shooting humans

There is more to this city
Than the blood splattered barrier that is around us

Hugo P. goes to Jovita Idar and has lived in Chicago from birth. He loves to write poems and sing songs. He wishes to be in a band as big as My Chemical Romance. He loves to draw as well. His favorite part of Chicago is all of Chicago. His least favorite songs are "I'm Not Okay", "Helena", and "Welcome to the Black Parade". He looks up to Gerard Way. He loves to read books. He sees himself as two different people: happy and sad. What he loves about the world is that he can be himself, but what he hates is that he will always be hated on. He loves the UFC and thinks people there are cool. He also loves WWE. His favorite color is black. He has a lot of friends but still has people who dislike him for who he his. He wants to fix himself as a person.

CHICAGO EXPERIENCE

BY CHARLIE V.

Skates grinding against the ice. Sticks hitting the puck. Coaches yelling. Fans cheering. The ding of the puck hitting the post. Bodies colliding. Refs whistling. Both teams talking back and forth to each other. Players arguing with the ref on a bad call or goal that was waved off. These are the sounds of a hockey game.

My team, the Cobras, has a game at South West Ice Arena against the Chicago Jets. Both my team and the Jets are triple AAA hockey teams. We are club teams, which means that we travel and are more competitive than high school teams. The players on the teams are from high schools that usually don't have hockey teams, or they don't want to play for their school. Students from those schools--Brother Rice, Mount Carmel, St. Rita, CHAS, Evergreen Park High School, etc.--come to play for a club team that is more competitive and faster than high school teams.

I wasn't able to play hockey at my school because it was a public school, and public schools don't normally have hockey teams because of the expense. A friend of mine told me about the Cobras and how it was a team that any kid from the area could join. So I went to tryouts and made the second highest team as a freshman. My team is a triple AAA team made up of freshmen, sophomores, juniors, and seniors. We all play well together and have no problem with each other. It's a fun team to be on.

We were at SIA and the game was about to begin. The players skated around on the ice, warming up and shooting pucks on the goalie. Both teams exchanged dirty looks. The Cobras and the Chicago Jets are rivals, two teams that don't like each other at all. I had never played this team because it was only my first year with the Cobras. I didn't know what to expect, how physical the team was going to be, if they hit a lot, if they were fast; I just didn't know. My coach pulled three of my teammates and me and asked us to protect our faster players and our goal scorers because the Jets hit a lot. These three guys and I were some of the bigger kids on my team, and the other team had at least six really big players. I was nervous because I didn't want to be the one to get hit and be hurt, but I had to protect my players.

During my second shift, my coach called me to the bench for a line change. While I was skating to the bench, I saw one of the bigger players coming down the side of the board with the puck, so I started to skate faster towards the player to hit him. He had his head down, and I hit him as hard as I could, shoulder to shoulder--a clean hit. The ref blew the whistle as the players from the other team started to push me and say stuff to me. The player I hit was hurt and stayed lying on the ice for two minutes before his teammates carried him off the ice to the locker room to be looked at to see if he was okay. The ref kicked me out of the game for hitting him while his head was down.

After the game ended, I went up to the player I had hit and apologized. His father saw me talking to him, ran over to separate us, and started yelling at me.

"Who do you think you are, hitting my son like that?" he yelled. "He could have gotten seriously hurt!"

"I'm sorry," I said calmly. "And I was just telling your son sorry."

"Shut the fuck up!" he replied.

My dad came over to us, clearly very angry.

"You can't talk to my son like that. He didn't mean to hurt your son," he told the man. "He said sorry to him and to you. It was a clean hit, and if you don't expect your kid to get hit like that, then don't have him play hockey."

This situation that happened to me didn't affect me and the sport I love at all. This kind of thing happens all the time in hockey games; it even happens in games with kids who are eight and nine. It happens a lot to everyone. After this happened, I didn't really take it personally, I just brushed it off. To this day, I still play and love the sport.

Charlie V. is eighteen years old. He grew up on the South Side of Chicago and is a senior in high school. He loves to play hockey and to watch his little brothers play hockey. He loves his family and friends. He loves to go fishing and spend time with his grandfather and uncle. He loves to teach his brothers everything he can to help them be better at hockey.

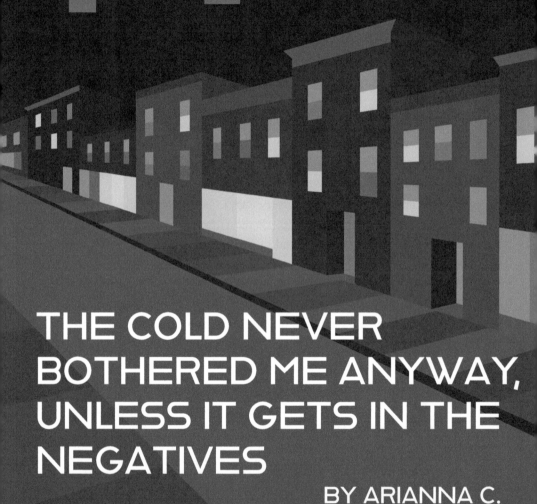

THE COLD NEVER BOTHERED ME ANYWAY, UNLESS IT GETS IN THE NEGATIVES

BY ARIANNA C.

In the cold night, the city lights illuminated the dark sky. The streets were crowded and there was a man playing a beautiful song on the saxophone on the street corner. Some people rushed past him to catch the train or to get home after a long day. Others stopped for a while and let the music take them over.

I was trying to get to the skating rink across the street but the music caught my attention, so I stayed back for a moment. I enjoyed the small performance taking place in the crowded streets. The music made me feel relaxed and at peace even though I was surrounded by a lot of noise and people. I felt warmth. Once the walk sign lit up, I crossed the street, hearing the deep rumbling of the train passing on the bridge above me. As I reached the other side I saw it: the McCormick Tribune ice rink.

The rink was full of people even though it was really cold. People as inexperienced as me held onto the rail as if holding on to dear life, meanwhile pros quickly traveled through the ice completely at ease. I couldn't help laughing when I saw some skaters slip and fall even though I was struggling myself, holding on to my cousin beside me. People, including myself, would fall and get back up laughing.

After some time of slipping and falling clumsily, I was getting the hang of it. My nose and ears were red and my fingers numb, but I was enjoying myself. I couldn't stop, I didn't want to. Everyone else around me looked like they felt the same way. No one wanted to regret anything once they left, so they decided to make the most of it while they could.

As I struggled through the ice I turned to the sound of loud cheering. When I turned I could see why: in the center of the rink there was a man kneeling in front of a flustered woman. In his hand I was able to see he was holding a ring. He slid it onto her finger and the crowd went wild. I felt happy for them, and apparently so did everyone else. Everyone clapped and congratulated the couple. I was fascinated at how we all felt comfortable with each other as if we were a whole family; I had noticed this long before the proposal. The crowd enjoyed the music together, the laughter that followed when someone slipped, the joy we all felt when we arrived, and the happiness that followed when someone went through an exciting time in their life.

We were all from different ethnicities, with different backgrounds and traditions, but that didn't seem to matter to anyone. We were all like a family, all of us in this city full of life called Chicago. When I was surrounded by these people, I didn't mind the cold.

Arianna C. is fourteen years of age and loves music and art. Her hobbies include drawing and playing a variety of instruments. She enjoys taking time to photograph anything she finds interesting. Arianna also takes inspiration from her photographs and surroundings. She has a pet fish that inspires her when drawing, he's a beautiful dark blue Betta fish that she loves.

COOLIN'

BY CARLOS P.

It was another summer day. The wind was cool, the street was silent, and the parking lot was hot. We were all playing football and about to go to Burger King. We were all loud, filling the street with laughter. We reached the main street and you could hear the cars roaring as they passed us. As we entered the Burger King, it was pretty awkward because there were ten of us in a fast food place. I ordered myself a ten piece chicken nuggets with a medium Sprite.

As we left, I got more Sprite. We went back outside and saw a Jewel Osco and decided to go in. We didn't have much of a purpose for going besides just fooling around. When we entered, we made a lot of noise so we would get kicked out but it never happened. Once we left the store, we saw two elderly men dressed up in fancy military uniforms with their medals who were asking for money. Three of my friends gave them money and they told us their stories. One of them served in the Air Force but I forgot the other one's story. As we were walking back to the parking lot, we all got thirsty because we were in a parking lot with no shade and we were playing football. Three of my friends went to a Walgreens that was nearby. When they came back, we all got water and refreshed ourselves.

After that we played a game that's like HORSE but with a soccer ball. You juggle it but if you drop the ball, you get a letter until you spell the word and then everyone playing has to shoot the ball at you. I was lucky because I was in a spot where no one would pass me the ball. I think it was the same person who always got hit. We played for an hour but then got bored and started to play catch until one of my friends punted my ball onto the roof of the building near the parking lot. That kind of annoyed me because that was the only football I had, but it was all good because I knew we weren't going to be able to get it. I also really didn't care because the football was ripped from the top and was scratched up. A couple of minutes later, my mom came to pick me up.

We went to Lindblom Park, which is close to our house. My brothers and I were riding our bikes and playing soccer with my dad which is always fun. We never really have time to be with him and this is a time when he is fun and not so serious. This was a special moment because he was actually happy and he looked like he was having fun playing with us. This is why I love my city, because it's not all violence like how our crazy president describes it. Chicago can also be a fun adventure that leads to good or bad. You will always leave satisfied by your experience. Even though my city is misunderstood by certain type of people, I still love Chicago.

Carlos P. is an eighth grader who goes to Jovita Idar. He has been living in Chicago ever since his momma gave birth to him. Carlos really enjoys roaming the streets of West Englewood were he lives. Carlos also wants to be a producer for upcoming artists in the rap game and give back to his parents for all they have ever done for him and give them a better life.

LOST

BY STANLEY G.

First time losing one of my homies

Man, it took a lot out of me

Blue and red lights all surround me

Tears of anger, sadness, revenge

Took over me

Ask God why it wasn't me

DONE THAT

Blood and tears, shed them all before

Greed and lust, fell for it all before

Friends and family, lost them all before

Crime and time, did it all before

But looking back, never did that at all before

HIS SAD SONG

Sing me a sad song about

A black kid with no home

Nowhere to go, no one to know

Hunger and hustle is all the boy knows

It's winter now and the boy

Lies dead in the snow

"Somebody help! Somebody help!"

Where was that about fifteen years ago?

Stanley G. is nineteen years old and has lived all over Chicago, so therefore he is very open-minded. Poems, visual arts, and music heavily influence him and have made a big impact on his life. At a young age, his experiences in Chicago have made an impact on the type of poems he writes, the type of art he draws, and the type of music he makes. He is very absorbent and his mind is complex.

BEYOND WHAT IT SEEMS

BY CYNTHIA M.

I woke up to a beautiful soothing song of Romeo Santos that made me want to dance. Automatically though, I knew in a Hispanic household that loud music meant cleaning. All day long. Getting over the displeased idea of cleaning, I walked out of my room. To my surprise I found no one. At that moment, I didn't really know whether or not to be relieved or worried that we weren't cleaning. My worry grew bigger and bigger as I seeked to find someone and I didn't. AHA! I'll follow the lovely sound of the music, which eventually dragged me outside. Once I opened the door, everything hit me all at once. Of course! JULY 24! The day of a block party.

Jumping with excitement, I knew today was going to be a great day from the jump. As I walked out BOOM it was almost like I was in paradise. I saw various types of mouth-watering foods like empanadas, tacos, gorditas, jumping houses, even loteria — all of that good stuff! Oh how I love block parties when the hot steamy sun touches my soft caramel skin and when I feel myself getting darker and darker, but none of that really matters to me when it's a block party.

Despite all the fun things at block parties, I absolutely love the people the most. As I walked down the block greeting everyone, I noticed everyone I knew was there: tías, tíos, cousins, neighbors...you name it. All the kids running around and their moms telling them to stop, threatening to take them home. Gosh, even the two drunk guys who stayed down the block at the corner were there. I loved seeing everyone living, escaping from all their problems. Block parties could make everyone fully enjoy themselves, even for one day out of the year at least. At a block party, it's not only about the kids, but the adults too. I love seeing everyone united, genuinely full of joy, like a utopia. That is the main reason why I love Chicago so dearly.

I open Twitter and see our "amazing" president making unreasonable statements like "Chicago is all violence" and see Instagram posts that say "Don't go to Chicago unless you tryna get shot." It frustrates me so much, to the point where I want to delete my social media, mainly because that's not the whole truth. Yes, Chicago has violence, but which place does not? People are too ignorant to acknowledge that maybe Chicago isn't what it seems, maybe there's another side they're not seeing. Truth being told, there is another side. And I want to welcome everyone to my side.

Chicago has graffiti, yes. Some of Chicago's neighborhoods don't look their best, yes. Chicago has violence, of course. But if you look a little closer and see the real meaning behind street art and see all the people together and united, I bet you'll want to come to Chicago — stop by block parties, visit The Bean, try Chicago's diverse foods. Do that, and I promise you'll love Chicago as much as I do.

Cynthia M. is a thirteen-year-old who was born and raised in South Side Chicago. She's very joyful, goofy, and energetic. Her favorite season is summer where she can play all her favorite sports like soccer, roller skating, volleyball, and fishing. She also enjoys playing Call of Duty when her older brother lets her, even though she's not very good at it. She hopes to be a therapist for teens and to be the first in her family to go to college.

FIRST LIFE LOVE

BY TYNASIA L.

The first time I felt love was the eighth grade. It happened when I was being myself. Based off my personality, somebody found it very interesting and liked me. I ended up finding out through a friend of that person. I gave that person a chance to make me happy and gave themselves a chance to do something right and make someone else happy. This person had a lot more in common with me than I thought. While I was getting closer with the mysterious person, we started hanging out and sharing and caring for one another.

April 13, 2017: We went to the AMC Classic Galewood Crossing 14. We were watching, holding hands, as I was getting nervous. Movie over, sneak and kiss, and then we were TOGETHER. That Monday, we came out in school, and everyone supported our relationship. We were finally a thang and I was actually happy with someone for once--taking me on dates, out to eat, and taking me to places that I'd love to go to or had never been before.

Tynasia L. (grade nine) is a fourteen year old female who attends Michele Clark Magnet school. She is a freshman in Chicago who plays basketball and hopefully will play in the WNBA as a future career. She quit the basketball team at her school-- she believes that she can get better at basketball on her own. She played on the best basketball team in the state, which was Marshall High School varsity team.

A MAGICAL CITY

BY CECILIA J.

As I looked out the window, it suddenly hit me. We were going to the beach for the first time this year! I quickly headed down the stairs to let my parents know I was awake. They seemed enthusiastic and ready for our beach day.

As we got in the car, I realized that it was a delightful, sunny day; it would be the perfect day to go to the beach. I was excited because it would be the first time in my life that I went to the beach with all my uncles and cousins. When we got to the beach, our whole family was happily waiting for us just as they said they would. I was thrilled to finally be able to get wet.

We cooked, talked, and played with so much joy that I could easily forget all my problems. It was amazing how we no longer cared about getting wet. We indulged in being able to spend time together and have fun, but most of all, in being with the people that we love.

When we were finally able to get in the water, it didn't matter to us that the water was awfully cold. All that really mattered was that we were all able to get in the water, play together, and have an astonishing day. This was the first time I realized how alluring the beach was. I was able to hear the waves moving and splashing against peoples' bodies. I heard the laughter, I heard the happiness it caused people to have. It was as if the water was not cold at all.

In that moment I knew what Chicago truly meant to me. It was glorious to see so many people full of joy. This showed me that it didn't matter if it was a perfect day to go to the beach or not. What really mattered was that everyone gathered there together.

All around me, all I saw were cheery parents with enchanted children, and even some with pleased dogs. I saw people on bikes, people taking pictures, and people simply having fun. Most of all I saw the people that made up Chicago, the people that made Chicago great. I noticed that somehow Chicago was able to provide people with happiness one way or another. It was able to provide different cultures, communities, families, friends, and everything that could make a person truly happy.

Chicago represents family and the power to unite everyone in Chicago to become a community, an alliance, a team. Chicago is capable of making families and relationships stronger and unforgettable. It doesn't matter where: the beach, the zoo, Navy Pier, it's all part of Chicago's magic and ability to create long lasting relationships. In Chicago, people are able to feel a kind if happiness that is contagious; no matter who you are, the joy will get you.

This is all what makes my Chicago the best place you would ever want to live. Chicago has always been a place full of joy; it's outstanding how much joy can go around from home to home, place to place. This has been possible because of all the people that cherish Chicago and make it feel alive. Chicago is home to many people who love and care for its beautiful landscapes and museums. Chicago has taught me to value many things such as family, culture, and diversity. Chicago has made me feel proud that I live here. I really don't know what I would do in a place other than Chicago. My Chicago is an inspiration.

Cecilia J. is a fourteen-year-old student at Jovita Idar Academy. She has lived in Chicago her whole life. She lives with her parents, brother, and sister. She has two dogs and really enjoys seeing the Chicago skyline. She really likes going to the beach and spending time with her family. She wants to be a successful doctor in the future. She hopes that she is able to travel to many places in the future such as Paris, Florida, and California.

LOLLAPALOOZA!

BY CHELSY L.

It was packed on the orange line
It felt tight
The closer we got to Grant Park
People were getting off
And people were coming in

Lollapalooza is when they're crazy
Jumping up and down, excitement exploding
Like the bass from speakers

The sun beat down on me
like the Sonoran desert
Machines encircled the crowd
Raining mist down on us
A cooling breeze in the melting heat
Air so refreshing

When 21 Savage came out
Screams erupted, like a savage tribe
Fans cheered "chee-hoo!"
Excitement dripping off of us like sweat

I got back to the train with excitement
The music still pulsing through my veins
Sleep would come late for me
As I replayed the day in my head
Memories turning to dreams

Chelsy L. is a student at Jovita Idar Academy. She is fourteen years old and has lived in Chicago for her whole life. She considers herself a makeup queen. She loves traveling to other places such as Texas and Mexico. She wishes to go to Puerto Rico and Columbia. She hopes to be an airline attendant in the future.

GO GET
EM, TIGER

BY MARIAH F.

Everyone has a journey, you know? A path where we choose which direction we want to go, what back roads we want to take, if we want to stand still or go as fast as we can. We don't choose where our journey begins, but as we all know, our life is ours alone. The decisions we make delineate what the accomplishments section of our eulogy says.

My journey began in a big city. A city where the winds run wild, as if engulfed in an intense game of tag. Where the sun sneaks a smile at you, then blushes and hides because the rain called dibs. Where you can't really see the stars at night, but understand that the city had to learn how to shine from somewhere.

This big city is Chicago. A place that warms my heart even though it has its cold nights. I'm not going to sit here and say that growing up in this city was hard, that the everyday intricacies that ABC Channel 7 News present is the epitome of my struggles. It's not. Is that still my Chicago though? It is. Every sidewalk, every corner, every alley defines where I come from, and where I come from is a part of who I am.

I grew up on the South Side of Chicago. I'm pretty sure if you walk along Western you'll find my name somewhere in the cement along the sidewalk. Not saying I put it there though. As a kid, I spent a lot of time sneaking out the house with my older brother and cousins, and I still do, sadly. Old habits, eh?

We would take off the chains on our imaginations and let them be free in a little neighborhood called Beverly Woods. We would find the craziest spots to climb when playing hide-and-seek and find the most outrageous lies to tell to cover up that we fell from that spot. We would go explore Kennedy Park after closing hours and mean mug the cops when they asked us to go home. To be honest, we got caught a couple of times by our parents, but that didn't stop us. The love for our city kept us going.

I remember when I was seven, my brother used to sneak out and steal our parents' car and we'd drive around the block, too scared to go too far. Now ten years later, I'm doing the same thing, but I'm scared that

I don't go far enough. I love driving with my friends, with a trunk full of sparkle fireworks, to the lakefront in the middle of October, where I'm embraced with familiar winds and bipolar weather. The feeling of the cold water drowning my feet, with the sparkles being the only thing I can see because it was one o'clock in the morning. Good times.

Growing up in Chicago has given me a sense of exploration. Indeed, I was born and raised here, but I don't want to stay here. I want to travel. I want to climb more questionable spots, I want to venture off after closing hours, I want to gaze at the sky to see if I see stars, before I decide to make my own with fireworks. Chicago has raised me and given me a kiss on my forehead, as if to say, "Go get 'em tiger." That's exactly what I plan to do.

Mariah F. is an eighteen-year-old obstreperous soul. Some say that God kissed the dirt she was made from, creating a blessed beauty. Others say that she's the first person to make him have his hands tied. Either/or, she's a lovable person.

DOWNTOWN MAGIC

BY NATALY D.

I remember it like it was yesterday. My family and I decided to stroll around downtown Chicago around 7:30 p.m. It was during the summertime, when the weather was just breezy and cool at night, and I had no worries about school the next day. I was wearing dark blue jean shorts, a yellow tank top, and my hair was in a bun. I always liked exploring downtown. I'd always admire the architecture and beautiful lights on the trees.

The first place we went to walk around was "The Cloud Gate." Or, as I like to call it, "el frijol." That's because it's shaped like a bean. I never really understood that art piece. I mean, why a shape of a bean, out of all the foods? I guess that's one of Chicago's unique elements. My legs grew sore from all the walking around. But I wasn't the only one. My family members said their legs were sore too.

In Chicago, there were people riding bike taxis. Fortunately for us and our feet, there was one near us. We called the driver over. He gave us a pleasant hello and we hopped into the back of his bike. It wasn't any ordinary bike, it was more of a carriage. The bike reminded me of how the pumpkin in Cinderella turned into a beautiful carriage. In this case, instead of a pumpkin it was a bike.

The young man brought us to the Buckingham Fountain. If you've never heard of it, it's a large gorgeous fountain in Chicago. At night, it looks magnificent with the lights in the water turning different colors. At the time, I never really found it interesting. I just thought it was a cool fountain.

That changed as I spotted this man behind me getting down on one knee and pulling out a decent-sized ring. At that very moment, I witnessed a proposal! Of course there were some heads turning and flashes from cameras. But I didn't notice any of that. I was just looking at the two partners' facial expressions. So much happiness and joy in one smile. It was such a mesmerizing moment.

When moments like that occur near you, you start to view some things differently, like the Buckingham Fountain its meaning. I didn't even know the couple, but I felt so much excitement for them because that moment of love happened here in Chicago, where I'm from. That's when I started to view my city as more than city full of great pizza and sports, but also a city full of love and new beginnings.

We finally arrived home in West Lawn. The lights looked like little clouds floating above the soccer field right across my house. We could hear people riding the squeaky swing sets at the park. Those sounds were a reminder that I finally got home. When I walked into my home I felt the warmth of my family and city .

Nataly D. is a fourteen-year-old. Chicago is her home. She loves soccer. In the future she's striving to be a psychologist and enjoys to eat at El Veneno with her family.

MY CHICAGO IS

BY LASHANTY N.

My Chicago is beautiful

My Chicago is big

My Chicago is home

My Chicago is sometimes dangerous

My Chicago is fun

My Chicago is for everyone

My Chicago is crowded

My Chicago is filled with restaurants

My Chicago is a city

My Chicago is fun to live in

My Chicago is a very friendly city

My Chicago is famous

My Chicago is filled with gang bangers

Lashanty N. is a fifteen-year-old girl. Lashanty's favorite colors are green and pink. She attends Michele Clark Magnet High School. What she likes best is track. Lashanty was born in Chicago, Illinois on February 21, 2003. She loves chitterlings and hot wings. She has two siblings: a sister and a brother. Lashanty was the only child for thirteen years. She plans on going to the Rio Olympics as one of her goals. Lashanty is very sweet, intelligent, brave, outgoing, pretty, and short. Her favorite movie is Joyful Noise.

SANDY SMILES OF CHICAGO

BY ELIZABETH T.

Every summer before the first day of school, my entire family heads to Chicago's famous Oak Street Beach. It has become a tradition for three years now and every year it's the same routine. Packing for the day at the beach is like being surrounded by wild animals fighting for their prey. My mom likes everything to be perfect; if we forget something it's "just not right," as my mom describes it. My family prepares a day in advance, it's like packing the entire house away for the day. We leave the car with just enough space for all of us to be seated and we head off to the beach.

Any Chicagoan knows how important it is to come early to everything because traffic and parking aren't one's best friend in the city. Finding parking in Chicago is, quite frankly, impossible, especially a free space. But for a day at the beach, it's totally worth the wait. We usually get the farthest parking spot, but we never complain.

We always find the perfect spot on the beach, with shade near enough to see Chicago's one-of-a-kind architecture. I admire the skyline, the variety of buildings in different shapes and sizes. Chicago not only has a diverse community, but the buildings are diverse as well. Observing the art in the sky has made me who I aspire to be, the sky being the limit to my goals. Chicago offers an infinite aspiration to all.

Every year, I start my new school year with all this encouragement. Chicago's art has had that impact on me. All the goals rush through me. I feel all the adrenaline because a day at the beach makes me feel capable for any challenge. Seeing what other people are capable of makes me who I aspire to be.

Once we settle in to our spot near the water, we start our annual cookout. Umbrellas bloom to cover the sun. Burgers and hotdogs are placed on the grill. We gather our table, preparing all the ingredients for the picnic. A day at the beach is nothing without bringing in my Hispanic culture. My dad grabs his mini speaker, the thing my mom dreads the most. "*Yo tenia mi cascabel, Con una cinta morada, Con una cinta morada, Yo tenia mi cascabel,*" my dad 'sings' yet it sounds more like he's yelling; he waits for us to respond to the chorus. She hates how my dad blares his music but I know he only does it because he is a full of joy, which I admire about him. We listen to mariachi music all day long, singing and dancing our souls out as if we were the only ones there. However, that couldn't be any farther from the truth. Hundreds of families, just like us, embracing their culture in their own way. Whether by their clothes, music, or language; Chicago is the place where we all fit in.

We end the day by going for a swim. The clear water is within reach. Seagulls fly side by side. Squealing children are running around the hot sand. The runners do their laps. Chants come from intense volleyball games. The beach is crowded, but that doesn't stop my family. Splashing wars come into play and we all fight until the end or at least when our eyes start to burn. The sun starts to dim down and that's our sign that it's time to go back home. We sit on the sand and dry off, reflecting on the glorious day we just had together. All the little things we ignore have had a major impact on me. Chicago's environment is what has made me who I am and I wouldn't ask for it any other way. Chicago is family. Chicago is diversity. Chicago is happiness.

Elizabeth T. is an eighth grader, fourteen years old, and attends Jovita Idar Academy on the South Side of Chicago, where she was born and raised. Elizabeth plays violin and is part of a community mariachi band, where she embraces her Latino culture. Elizabeth loves burgers, pancakes, and chicken nuggets; if she had the option, she'd eat them everyday. She wants to become an attorney and have her own law firm in the future. Elizabeth plans to attend Lane Tech for the upcoming year and be able to travel the world.

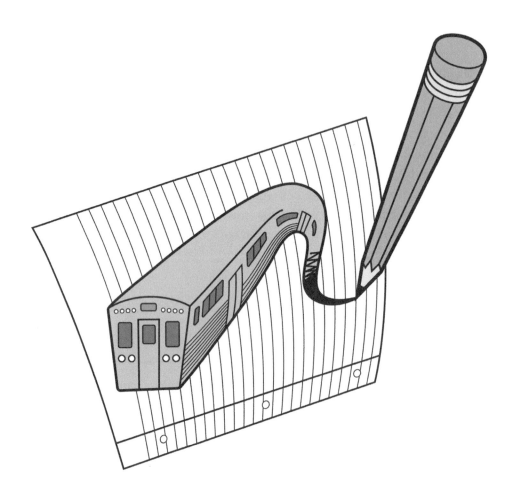

WRITING PROMPT 4:

Pick one to free write about.

A. What's a story that comes to mind about your experience with schools in Chicago?

B. Where have you found love in Chicago?

C. Where do you find your voice in Chicago?
Where do you find freedom in Chicago?

THE GLOWING

PARKS OF CHICAGO

BY LUIS P.

Chicago is a beautiful place and the parks are as well.

Whether you go to Seneca or Marquette Park,

There is always somewhere to play in the park.

I personally go to Lindblom Park, I always see people in it.

People play basketball and I always hear kids screaming out of joy.

In the summer the park is always active, there's a field that people play in.

The grass is always green and it looks very clean.

The sun glows down at the park and it makes it look pretty.

The ice cream truck tunes get all the little kids' attention.

I go there everyday in the summer and I play soccer with my dad and my brothers.

We joke around when we play but we can be competitive sometimes.

The parks here are beautiful, you don't want to miss out on them.

If you come to Chicago, make sure to visit one of these beautiful parks.

Luis P. is a young fourteen-year-old teenager that goes to school at Jovita Idar Academy. Next year he will be attempting to attend Cristo Rey Jesuit High School. His favorite color is blue and he has a twin brother. He likes to play soccer and football with his neighbors in the summer. He enjoys playing video games in his free time. He likes being positive and keeping good vibes.

CITY OF DREAMS

BY DAVID C.

Ever since my brother graduated from Lane Tech College Prep, It's been one of my greatest dreams to get accepted to Lane. It was a bright, sunny, but chilly Saturday morning in Chicago. My parents and I were waiting in line for doors to open for Lane Tech's open house. As I stood in the magnificent line of a ton of people, I noticed all of them. I noticed all the people around me were from all different ethnicities.

Everyone had something unique about them. Everyone had their own style, their own voice and personality, but we had something in common. We all wanted Lane Tech to be the place where all our dreams come true. Finally, after a couple of minutes we were next in line to enter the school. As my parents and I entered the incredible auditorium, I could see magnificent white walls with a never-ending amount of chairs. My adrenaline started to flow through my body faster and faster as I saw all the options Lane Tech had to offer. Music of all different cultures were played, sang, and danced to by the students of Lane Tech. The audience, including myself, was amazed by the presentations. The applause from the crowd just grew louder and louder.

The music and presentations stopped and green flags were waved in the air, indicating it was time to start exploring the school. We exited the auditorium with our small group and mentor. We started walking down the enormous and crowded hallways. Everyone was divided into groups. At every corner of the hallway there was a stand showing different knowledge and experiences that Lane Tech had to offer, with hundreds of clubs for everyone. The demonstration of all these different clubs and experiences inspired me to try new things that I've never really tried, like dancing or playing music from different cultures.

Going to the Lane Tech open house inspired me to believe that anything is possible. I could see guitar players that could fill dozens of rooms. I could see artists of the future, the journalists that we will hear or read about in ten years, the designers that will create different styles of clothes or that will design buildings and skyscrapers in our own Chicago skyline.

You might know Chicago as the place of hot dogs and deep dish pizza or an awesome skyline, but we are so much more. Chicago is where everyone is included despite our many differences. Chicago has a place for all of us to belong and succeed. Chicago is the place, where we receive an endless amount of opportunity. We decide our futures and what we want to accomplish in our lives without those chances or opportunities being lost no matter what gender, religion, or ethnicity we are.

David C. is a thirteen-almost-fourteen-year-old teenager who is attending Jovita Idar Academy middle school. David has lived in Chicago his whole life. He is active in sports (soccer) and music (mariachi) in and outside of school. He's played soccer almost all his life and has been playing music since fifth grade. He hopes to continue doing these things and maybe even start a career with them.

CHICAGO'S
BEST THINGS

BY JUAN M.

When I am in Chicago it feels like my homeland,
where I always spend all of the time and it is really fun to be here.
When I am downtown there are just a lot of things to do,
I don't ever want to leave.
There are a lot of stores in Chicago.
My favorites are GameStop and Target or like Dick's Sporting Goods,
it's just really fun because there are a lot of stores.
You should go there to find out what they are.
Most of my time to I spend playing video games like Halo, Call of
Duty, and some Injustice 2,
just really cool games over all.
There are so many good places to go eat.
My favorite place is Manolo's Tamales.
I go there almost every Sunday to eat in the morning.
It is really great and the tamales verdes are my favorite.
It's really cool that I have a lot of places to go to eat like Paco's Tacos.
It's a good place too, not my favorite, but a really nice place to eat
tacos de carne asada.
One big thing in Chicago for me is that almost all of my family lives
here.

Juan M. has lived in Chicago for thirteen—about to be fourteen—years. He likes to play sports but sometimes it is cold and he'll just play some Call of Duty. His favorite place to be in Chicago is downtown, there are really great stores. He lives with his parents in Chicago. Juan likes the Percy Jackson book series and his favorite movie is Black Panther.

WHERE I
FOUND LOVE
IN CHICAGO

BY DARRYL D.

I found real love from my best friend. I met her five years ago when she was in eighth grade and I was in seventh grade. I met her in the summer near 64th and Drexel. My friend and I were just walking when he saw her. They started talking, then I asked who she was. He told me to go see and talk to her. My first thought when I walked up was, Wow, she's short and beautiful with glasses. I wonder, is she taken or single? I introduced myself, and we talked about how old she was, what school she went to, and what made her happy. I asked for her number, and she said she would text me the day, but I didn't believe it She told me her name was Kytiana.

The next day, I was just chilling in my house when I heard my phone ring. It was a message from Kytiana. The message said, "I need to get myself together. I'm not ready for a relationship." I felt a little bit sad, but I wasn't hurt. I didn't really know her. Even though she wasn't ready for a relationship, we became friends. She lived up the street from me on 64th and Ellis, and we saw each other every day. We got to talking, and she came to know me like I know the back of my hand. I realized what a loving, beautiful girl she was, and as we got closer and closer, I saw what a caring heart she had.

The most exciting day was when I made her my girlfriend. We had been friends for four years when I asked her to be my girlfriend. I felt so confident about it. I thought we were going to last forever just because the way we used to vibe was so perfect. We told each other everything and never lied to one another. When we took a break from each other, she always gave me a second chance, even a third chance. She had my back forever, and I had hers. She loved me like no other. I loved her. Everything was just perfect until she changed on me.

The craziest thing happened on New Year's Eve. I went to a party in Indianapolis, and when I came back to my phone, I saw a text from her saying that she didn't want a relationship. So I thought to myself, All those sweet things she were saying, and saying she wouldn't change on me, were those lies? We talked that night and ended up agreeing to stay together. Later that night, at 2:53 a.m., she texted me saying she was sorry but she couldn't do this anymore. I just left it alone. She gave me my clothes back, and we never talked again .

What I learned from this was no matter how long you know someone, he or she can change on you like there's no tomorrow, even the people you knew the longest. I loved Kytiana when I thought I knew who she was, but now I don't care about her or what she has going on in her life. I wouldn't wish this pain on my worst enemy, but I learned never to trust anyone. Words are just words, and actions speak louder than them. Even though a person can say things to make you fall in love with them and their words, you shouldn't believe it until they show it.

Darryl D. is nineteen years old and grew up in Chicago. He is very social and enjoys basketball, music, and photography.

INTO THE WILD

BY PETER ALEXANDER R.

Here in the streets, Americanized
Raised in the city where I'm living in lies
Grab you by the collar, but I don't know why
Cause they'll pull you to jail, just to take you apart

Even though you don't see what I see
Well, you don't know

Well, I see you while you stand there
Junkies and real drunks there
Well, leaving Chicago ain't easy
Well, I've got to drop out
I've got to jump out
Well, let's dance in your apartment
I'm leaving just to get there
Well, she's coked out in December
Well, I've got to get out
I've got to run now
But when I try to skip town
Lake Michigan's around
And I'm drunk every night
With my friends driving around

Well, stuck in Chicago
Concrete and no goals
I hate you so much
The Windy City
It robs you of your dreams
I hate you so much

Well, I'll run you down
Just to shoot you down

They say you're of age
But they don't mean now

Yes, I'm trying
But I don't mean now
And I guess I'll stay a while
Cause I can't leave now

Sometimes in your eyes
Slow me down but don't tell me why

Well, I see you while you stand there
Junkies and real drunks there
Well, leaving Chicago ain't easy
Well, I've got to drive fast
And this city won't last
Well, let's dance in your apartment
I'm driving just to get there
Well, she's coked out in December
Well, I came to come clean
It's the drugs, it's not me

And I'm out every night
On the street, wandering around

Well, stuck in Chicago
City of broken homes
I hate you so much
Stuck in Chicago
Stuck in Chicago
Stuck in Chicago
They hate you so much.

Peter R. is a graduating senior at Pathways in Education: Ashburn. Peter is a persistent pioneer of the urban frontier. He is a relentless reader, a maverick musician, and a passionate poet. He is the student that you simply admire, and an individual who can give a compass its direction.

MY CHICAGO MEMOIR

BY SHARONDA J.

It was a bright July. Summer, sun beaming so nice: my eleventh birthday, my first house party barbecue. All my friends were drowning me with love and happiness. I ran up and down Gladys Street in West Garfield Park with my friends with my pink, white, clear, and black beads shaking making all the noise that I couldn't even hear. I took a break and ran to my backyard to ask my dad how the food was coming along, as he flipped the the barbecued hamburgers, ribs, and hotdogs on the grill. It smelled like the best barbecue in the world.

My dad said, "Yeah, sugar, it's going good. Is you enjoying yourself?"

I answered, "Yes."

I ran back outside and played more games and danced all day. My mom called me in and said, "It's time, sugar."

I ran upstairs, all my friends stood around me and my Diego cake as I laughed and got ready to sing. My sister was snapping pictures like crazy. I blew out candles, I wished that I could have another birthday like this again. I cut my cake and ran outside and had the best time ever. At the beginning of the day, I thought this day would be the worst day ever because I wanted to do something else, but I had an amazing birthday. This birthday was an important one because my whole family and neighborhood came over. This day showed how my family gets together to celebrate family. It's all about making the worst things that happen into good. And that's what I did.

Sharonda J. is a ninth grader at Michele Clark High School. She was born the day before the Fourth of July and she enjoys her birthday every year. She loves to dance; it's her passion. She wants to be a neonatal nurse and have a celebration party. She loves all types of music and she can dance to all types of music. She is the best counselor you can talk to cause she's been through it all. She loves sherbert ice cream and if she's not in the mood or not being herself, give her an Italian beef or chocolate, she will be happy in seconds.

THE DIFFERENT
TASTES OF CHICAGO

BY ELIAS G.

At the Taste of Chicago
the food is so great
that you would even want some tomorrow
but it only lasts a day

At the end of the day
you are so full
but you pray
for another handful

You see all types of restaurants
now we must have the best food
and I don't want to taunt
'cause I don't want to start a feud

You see all the smoke
you smell all the meat
you just want a coke
but all you can do is eat

You feel the sun burning your skin
you go under the tents for some shade
you feel the food on your chin
so you reach for some Gatorade

You go to the train
you see people eating their food
you make sure you walk on the right lane
then you go home in a good mood

Elias Ismael G. is thirteen years old and attends Jovita Idar Academy. He loves to play sports, mostly basketball. He loves to play video games. He will literally know every new game coming out. He is really good at math and basketball. When Elias is older he wants to be a software designer. He has lived in Chicago for ten years. He loves it there.

MY OTHER WORLD

BY ANA B.

The day was very sunny and I could see the trees through the window of my room. My uncles decided to take my sisters and me to downtown Chicago. As we drove, I looked at the trees with their beautiful flowers. When we arrived downtown, I was very surprised to see all the buildings with their bright lights, trains passing by above the cars, and the sky looked different from other parts. I had never seen a place with so many buildings full of beautiful lights. Other buildings were strange shapes like diamonds. My sister and I took many pictures. I liked the Bean, the tower that throws water, and the fountain with spectacles of lights.

Chicago became a very important place for me. We walked towards a music presentation with violins and guitars playing joyful songs. Everything was very beautiful. My sister and I were very delighted by what happened that day and what we saw. I do not regret having come to this country. It is so beautiful and safe. I would like for other people to come visit this country, to have this beautiful experience that I had with Chicago. I hope that the people who enter Chicago feel very welcome, just as I felt, and they see how beautiful Chicago is.

Chicago has become something that I appreciate a lot and has become part of my life. Even if the president only says bad things about Chicago, that does not really define what Chicago is. I am proud to be one more inhabitant in this beautiful city—CHICAGO.

Ana B. is a fourteen-year-old eighth grader at Jovita Idar Academy. She moved from Honduras to Chicago with her two sisters when she was twelve years old. She lives with her uncles, two sisters, and three cousins. At the moment, Ana only speaks spanish. She likes to read, her favorite sport is soccer, and one of the things she likes about Chicago is the Bean because she finds it really funny-it's almost like a optical illusion.

SKY HIGH

BY JORGE F.

It was a bright sunny day out in downtown Chicago. The breeze I felt as we drove down the streets was like opening the freezer at home. My siblings, father, and I were excited because we were heading to the John Hancock building. I had never been ninety-six stories high up above the ground before and the thought of that made me nervous, but nevertheless I was thrilled to see where this could go.

While in the car, we listened to rap music, specifically music by Migos as that's what my brother preferred. As I looked out the window I could see the various shops that downtown has to offer like Forever 21, Adidas, Gucci, and Champs. I always thought it would be cool to own a company like that and earn lots of money, and maybe someday I could be Bill Gates or Elon Musk leading the world of technology towards the future.

So when we finally got to the John Hancock Building parking lot we weren't sure what we would eat after we came back down. We decided to have lunch after coming down from the observatory. As we entered the building there was a huge line to go up to the observatory. While we were waiting, there was a kid who was about nine years old throwing a fit because there were too many people ahead of him.

We finally were able to get through the line and as we walked towards the elevator we saw tons of pictures with Chicago's history everywhere. I was amazed at every little fact there was including the structure of the John Hancock Building and how many years it took to construct it. All this history was helpful because it kept us occupied as we waited in line for the elevator.

When we made it to the elevator, we were excited that we were finally going to be in the high rise. Entering the elevator, I didn't like how it was packed with about twenty people, but the wait was almost over. Going up floor by floor I started to feel this obnoxious buzzing in my ears. So as we stepped out of the elevator I raced to the windows and the view was incredible!

First I looked at the east side and I could see Lake Michigan stretching out for miles. The lake had this light and dark blue pattern including sky and cerulean blue in it. Then I looked towards the west side and it was amazing. I could see Midway Airport near where I live. I could see all the surrounding neighborhoods. And the north was probably my favorite because I could see all the skyscrapers and parks that make Chicago what it is. To me, the north resembles Chicago the most because I think Chicago is all about the sky-high buildings and the north side reminded me of that.

As we left the building and drove back home, I started to feel inferior in some way. Being up ninety-six stories in the sky made me feel like I was in power and I had never felt something like that before. The experience was amazing and maybe I can go to the John Hancock Building again.

Jorge F. is a fourteen-year-old who loves playing video games and watching The Flash. As he gets older he is thinking about following a career in professional gaming. He isn't much of an outgoing person and would rather be inside most of the time. He attends Jovita Idar Academy as an eighth grader and will be entering high school in 2018. Currently he lives with his mother, brother, and sister in Chicago, Illinois.

MY HOME

BY KEVIN H.

Chicago isn't a place,
It's a home to anyone willing to join its community.
Our community can't be broken, yet it can be fixed.
It isn't perfect but there is always room for improvement,
As we have our ups and downs.
But we do have a city filled with businesses,
Crowds swarming the streets of the Windy City,
Passing through or visiting our best spots.
Chicago has big shoulders
Waiting for anyone to come lean on.

Kevin H. is thirteen years old, but wants to be clear he will be turning fourteen really soon. He's an alright lad, although he tends to get into a bit of mischief, which may not always be the best thing, according to the mischief-maker himself. He's lived in Chicago his entire life, although he does hope to travel one day. He'd like to be a detective when he grows up, because he wants to help others and bring bad guys to justice. Or, maybe a comedian - he loves having a laugh or getting a laugh from someone; Kevin feels best when making other people smile.

CHICAGO
REIMAGINED

BY RILEY T.

United we stand, divided we fall,

As they say.

But how are two-sided discussions running my city?

We shall come together as Honest Abe did,

What a great man he was,

To take lesser and make greater and equal.

We are savages as wild as bulls ravaging ancient cookware.

There are no quiet nights here in this city,

Sirens

Laughter

Gunshots

Screams

Yelps

Traffic,

From one violent block to another civilized.

My city roars with compassion and pride,

Where men can fight but come together to watch their team.

As Lithuanian ancestors honored the strong movements of their family before them,

Keeping pride alive.

Gunmen roam, right to family and wrong to public.

What is that algorithmic logic?

You can smell the foul taste, explicit

Where they say it's better than undone.

They say enterprises shall relinquish a man's will to be powered.

The streets are hyenas, sneering at us as we walk free.

Give a man a dollar and he'll give it away.

Give a woman a dollar and she'll help.

We are this, the Land of Lincoln where violence hides in corners.

When you grow up on these blocks, you're built for them.
Speak freely
Think wittingly
Stand up
In the big bad city -
Chicago.

Riley T. is eighteen years old and grew up on the South Side of Chicago. She developed her passion for writing at a very young age. She read all seven Harry Potter books in three months when she was twelve. She has her very own poetry book in the works, soon to be self-published, with hopes that it will lead her somewhere. She's a self-taught photographer and has a love for taking pictures with strong meaning. She's currently applying for scholarships to get into her dream school in Boulder, where she hopes to pursue her passion of literature, English, and photography to land her dream job as a photojournalist or teacher.

WRIGLEY FIELD

BY ANTONIO G.

A swarm of red, white, and blue
Swells through the stands,
A sea of pride.
You would think it's the 4th of July,
But really you're at the friendly confines
Of Wrigley Field where people
Share the same passion as you,
Loving the Chicago Cubs.

My grandparents inspired my love for the Cubs.
My first game ever at the age of four
I will never forget, even if I didn't understand the game,
Thanks to the cheering after a home run.
Meeting Clark the Cub,
 Nothing was better than singing out
"Go Cubs Go"

Going to Wrigley Field is a feeling you will never forget.
You will get goosebumps
Once you are in the environment of Wrigley Field.
The energy is really great,
Nothing makes you feel more welcome.
Seeing the merchandise people
Selling cubs merchandise and screaming out,
The fans chanting
"Go Cubs Go"

Once you walk into Wrigley Field, the place will take you away.
The feeling you get is unforgettable.
Going to Wrigley Field will change your life.

Even to this day, me and my grandparents go to Cubs games.
Now I share a love for the Cubs more than I used to,
Now I know the game more than I used to.

The first time I went to Wrigley Field,
I discovered my passion.
I will love playing baseball and be proud to live in my city.
Chicago is where my dreams began.

Antonio (Tony) G. is a fourteen-year-old male who lives in Chicago. He enjoys sports, mostly baseball and basketball. He likes to play Fortnite in his spare time. He is a Cubs superfan, catch him at Wrigley Field.

MEMOIR OF CHICAGO

BY PAOLO S.

As I walked around downtown Chicago, I remembered hearing lots of clicking and flashing noises everywhere. The tourists were walking around taking so many pictures. Click! Click! Flash! Flash! They were all admiring the tall and enormous buildings. My family and I decided to do the same thing. We went sightseeing downtown. I remember looking up and seeing how enormous the buildings were. They went up so high in the blue sky clouds. I remember my neck hurt from looking so high up!

First, I visited the Willis Tower and it was scary just looking down all the crystal clear windows. I felt like I was going to fall! We took the elevator up to see the city from way up high. Then, I saw the John Hancock building, which was very similar to the Willis Tower because of its similar color. The only unique difference I noticed between the buildings was the John Hancock building's long antennae.

Next, I took pictures of the distinct art sculptures from the museums. They were all interesting with unique designs. Visiting downtown, I discovered that Chicago has such rich architecture that goes all the way back to the 1900s. Chicago's architecture has very eye-catching detailed designs. In fact, some of these buildings are city landmarks representing a specific time in history. Because I really like history, this is one of the reasons why I love Chicago's buildings and coming downtown was a way for me to admire it all. I especially liked the sophisticated architecture of the Water Tower, the shiny silver Bean, and the art museum with two immense lions at the main entrance.

I was ecstatic to be with my mom, dad, and younger brother. It was a great experience for me because I was able to see so much and spend time with my family. I had lots of fun, and then we went out to eat delicious food downtown.

After eating, I also observed just how entertaining the downtown area is for its many diverse visitors. People everywhere were enjoying their walks, shopping, eating, taking pictures, and most of all enjoying this beautiful city of Chicago. In addition to the buildings, I was able to see the easily accessible CTA train. It was fun taking a tour in my city!

There is a lot to say but…

Ooh! I almost forgot! The Millenium Park was the most enjoyable for my family and me. I especially loved the park and walking on the side of Lake Michigan. I felt the lake's breeze and saw the crystal blue water waves as I walked along the lake's walkway. For these reasons, I have to say that Chicago is an awesome city to live in. Lastly, I highly recommend visiting this city especially in the summertime. It will surprise you!

Paolo S. is a thirteen-year-old adolescent who enjoys playing the violin and loves listening to different genres of music. He especially enjoys learning all about unique skyscrapers and is very open to learning new things. Science and math are his favorite subjects because they are his strengths in school. On the other hand, he dislikes constant repetitive questioning because he finds it frustrating and prefers straight forward conversation. In his free time, he likes to ride his bicycle and also loves to play baseball outside. In fact, he is quite a good pitcher and batter. He also enjoys staying at home during his summer break. However, he is ecstatic about going to different places with his family when possible and he likes to enjoy, enjoy, enjoy.

MY CHICAGO

BY DARRELL T.

What angers me about Chicago

The tension builds inside of me when the news informs us about the gun violence. This is a big problem because people are becoming afraid to go outside. I remember when you could walk outside without having to mind your surroundings and be unafraid. I wish Chicago could go back to around 2004 when there was less gun violence around the city.

The future of Chicago

I stand here looking ahead to the future in Chicago: I can see there is less gun violence in Chicago and people are not afraid to come outside. The gas prices around the city are lower so people can save up money and the food prices are also low. The crime rate went down a lot thanks to less gun violence around the city.

Cloud Gate

It was my first time going downtown when I was thirteen years old. My mom drove my brother and me there on Lake Shore Drive. My brother, my mom, and I walked to the silver big bean statue known as the Cloud Gate. It was loud and there were a lot of people walking around us. It made me feel a little happy while smelling the clean fresh air. Remembering this makes me happy.

CPS and Love

When I first start going to school in Chicago, I started to notice that I'm really good at making friends with my teachers, thanks to the kindness of my grandma. The teachers at every school always have smiles on their faces when they see me. Sometimes, I talk to them about my time in other schools and about home.

I first found my love in Chicago and it is video games. When I was six my mom was playing Mario Bros 3. She passed the controller to me so I could play with my brother and once I started playing I couldn't stop.

This is how I found my love in Chicago: playing video games.

I first found my voice in Chicago at Pathways. This school made me feel the way it should at all schools. It's not loud, the students are nice, and the teachers make sure you get the help you need in order to get done with your work. I first found my freedom in United States of America; it is the land of the free after all!

Darrell T. is addicted to pizza Pringles. He is serious about doing work. Darrell wants you to know that the teachers at Pathways are very kind and nice. He is 21 years old. He is very kind to students and teachers. He loves to play video games 24/7.

THE
BLINDING LIGHT

BY AXEL R.

The
blinding light shines throughout the shore
The laughter of people heard across the lake

The shade cools while the sun burns

You hear the leaves of the trees shaking

You see planes above you making the loudest roar

The skyline of a city filled with beauty

Your loved ones are smiling
others are relaxing in the shade

You and your cousins are in the water
Laughing about the world around you
You two are splashing water at each other like it's the last day on earth
Your mom, dad, and siblings are having a picnic on the sand

you can tell

everyone
there
is happy

Axel R. goes to Jovita Idar Academy in Chicago, Illinois. His favorite spot in Chicago is his neighborhood park, Senka Park. His hobbies are drawing, reading and sleeping. His favorite book series is the Percy Jackson series and his favorite movies are monster flicks like Gojira. He aspires to be either an author or a visual artist.

NAVY PIER
IMPACT

BY NICK S. P.

Navy Pier: a place to have fun, socialize, have more fun, and be with your family.

It illuminates you just like in the dark when you find light.

We were family walking down in the hot sun. The breeze blew cool air, but the sun warmed us up like nothing had happened.

When we went to eat at Bubba Gump, they were serving mariscos and my family had clams to eat. When my sister tried to slurp it, it made her almost choke and we were all having a good laugh like it was karma. We were really trying to have fun. It made us feel bad but it was still a good laugh.

Navy Pier has a mall so big that I didn't know where to start, but I had my family to help guide me through.

As we were walking down the sidewalk and we were talking to another family, my mom noticed that my little sister wasn't there. We all freaked out and we were scanning to see if she was in a store. My dad called to the front of the pier where there was a speaker and they told him they would send a warning that a little girl with ponytails and a blue shirt with a butterfly on it was missing.

Finally, somebody saw her at a shop buying some candy and we felt a relief like the day had loosened up. We felt like it was God's will that let us find her. We were mad at her at first but we felt so happy that we had found her again.

You have the opportunity to relax and just enjoy yourself and get to explore how amazing it is, especially on the Fourth of July.

It's like if you are in a big, humongous family and it's really good because all of us were chatting and we were eating some snacks. Everybody was so excited to see the parade of fireworks.

Everybody got quiet for a few moments and waited patiently as if there was someone in your back making you feel the goosebumps.

It was like shooting stars in a festival of exploding in a middle and like it felt like if they were having a fiesta over there as it sparkled through my eyes like if it was candy for my eyes.

As one was turning down, another one raised itself and I felt a satisfaction on my heart. It looked like there was a diamond in the sky shattering into a million pieces.

We said goodbye to all the people we had met and headed home.

This was a really memorable experience because we were with our family. We had all of our adventures and different emotions and it was what really felt my Chicago for me and maybe for you too.

Nick S. P. is a thirteen-year-old student at Jovita Idar Academy. He is really good at sports, learns quickly and does well in math. He is a very friendly person to meet. He loves ice cream. He rides horses as a hobby. His favorite TV show is *Rick & Morty* and he enjoys society just the way it is. He lives with his family and hopes to someday be a doctor.

FINDING
MY VOICE

BY DEANNA D.

I experienced so many things in Chicago just by finding my voice, dealing with school, and finding love. Dealing with school was always a struggle because people used to bully me and make fun of me when I was younger. I never really caught on as quick as others did. I also used to let people's words about me get the best of me. Now, looking back, I know I shouldn't have let that get to me.

I never really liked math because, honestly, I always failed in it. As I got to high school, I always dealt with people who would always piss me off and I would end up in fights. But, my last high school fight was in December of 2016. I've improved in so many ways. It's so incredible I would have never thought I would be the one to change my ways.

I did it for a good cause though. My sophomore year of high school I found love with this amazing guy. He was everything I ever wanted in a boy. He was sweet, cute, and funny. He was also nice to me. I loved him because of how he treated me; he never judged me or talked bad about me. Finding love was amazing because I finally found somebody who I connected with; Xavier was my biggest supporter. He stood by me when no one else did. He always told me that I'm going to be great and I have a voice that everyone is going to listen to. Xavier was a wonderful person and my best friend. He gave me the best advice to always be myself and speak out when I really need to, but by then the relationship was ending. We've stayed friends after the break-up. He is still standing by my side and telling me to never doubt myself and always be the best person I can be.

I found my own voice and self-confidence when I was at school and I saw that I was succeeding and seeing improvement in my work and myself. I decided to become and always be different than others. I've learned it's always okay to be yourself and never change who you are because somebody wants to make you change. Never follow in the footsteps of others; be a leader. That's what I always stood by and I feel as though if I show others that I have a voice they can do the same and speak out and speak up.

Deanna D. is eighteen years of age. Growing up she's always been through the struggle and has always been sick. Deanna has always been the girl who was judged because of how she looked and the way she dressed. People used to say she dressed like a boy because she used to always wear Jordan's. Deanna is only 4'10", very short. Deanna honestly never used to like school cause she always found it boring. But she had goals in life, and she needed to succeed in life. Deanna's hobbies are writing, dancing, and playing the game sometimes. She is such a happy, outspoken, and adventurous girl. Deanna's goal in life is to becoming a doctor who works with kids and take care of them.

THE
OTHER SIDE

BY LUIS V.

The sun has set, the fireflies come out with their beautiful green light. The crickets start chirping. I'm six years old and I'm wearing my favorite shirt. I'm outside in my front yard with my neighbor, we're kids. We like the cold and fresh air hitting our sweaty faces while running. We are having a good time until we start hearing shooting. We start running inside and hide under my bed. That's how life is in the South Side of Chicago.

There is never a day without a person being killed or going missing. My family is afraid of being in that situation. My mom is afraid of losing my brothers and me but we can't afford to live on the North Side.

One day, I was at the store with my mom. I was only two years old and a guy tried to kidnap me but a cop stopped him before it was to late. After that day, my mom has been more strict so she can never lose us or see us as gangsters.

My family has gone through a lot before and after I was born, but we have each other to be happy. The South is not a safe place, but downtown is so beautiful, the only thing I do is stare outside the window and be amazed by the tall buildings and the strange structures. Sometimes when I leave Chicago and return, I can't believe I live in this amazing city.

The South is pretty much the poor side and the North is the rich. I remember my brothers and I saying we will live in a huge mansion with a pool, but seeing how life is right now, I don't think I'll be living in a mansion any time soon.

The schools in Chicago can be horrible or wonderful. I used to go to a school where gangs were outside in the playground trying to pick a fight with the older kids, but today I'm lucky enough to be in one of the coolest looking schools in Chicago. My school is mostly steel and blue glass. We also have amazing teachers that actually care about the students.

I remember my mom telling me to get good grades because we can't afford to pay for college, after that I tried, but sixth grade is the year I started getting C's and D's. But high school will be a new start for me.

I want to do great things in Chicago, I want to make a difference in the South. That's one of my goals: to change the South to be more like the North. How I'm going to do that is by being a police officer, to change the way life is in the South and stop crime.

I'm proud of living in Chicago. Michael Jordan one of the most famous basketball players who ever lived and he played for the Bulls. The first black president is from Chicago. One of the best rappers — Chance The Rapper — is from Chicago. We also have the best hockey team, the Blackhawks.

The things I'm not proud of is how the Bears and the Bulls are always losing.

Life in Chicago is not that different from other cities, the rich live in the cool looking buildings, the poor live in the poor neighborhood. Each city has its unique thing like museums and buildings. They also have their negatives. Chicago has a lot of killing.

My favorite thing about Chicago is that Transformers 4 was filmed here, that's pretty amazing.

Luis V. was born and raised in Chicago. In 2011-2018, he went to Jovita Idar Academy. He's a third degree black belt in Tae Kwon Do. He's also a huge gamer and loves the Maze Runner series. He also enjoys hanging out with his friends.

THE TRUE
CHICAGO

BY STEVEN S.

The story starts on a nice beautiful bright sunny day. We have three total families, my family, and two other families that are my cousins. We all met at the CTA Western orange Line train stop. Everyone in Chicago takes the train because it's like the mighty oak tree, no matter how old they get, they will always be strong.

After we get off the train, we see all of these really tall old buildings with lots of rich history. When people think of skyscrapers, I don't believe that they think of Chicago. I don't think people really know that skyscrapers were originally made in Chicago.

Chicago is the only place I know so far where you have all of these buildings and instantly get hit by all of this nature all around you. Our first destination was a walk near the lake. Everyone was split into two groups: one group was the adults and the other was the group of kids. Everyone was chatting along about different things like dresses, videogames, etc. while looking at the beautiful scenery and the boats in the water. At one point we even saw a pirate ship. Everyone was happy and having a great time. But the day was still not over, and it was time for the next place.

We stopped to eat near Buckingham Fountain. While eating, everyone kept chatting along about other fun times we have had before, but when I finished I walked to the fountain. I can still remember the first time I saw the fountain when I was about five. The fountain still looks the same. It's like no matter how big you get you will always look like an ant compared to it. I went back to stand with my family and eventually we all went to the fountain as a group.

From there, we went to Crown Fountain. Crown Fountain looks like two massive dominos that are separated. Images are projected on one side of it. The picture is always an image of people's face that shoots out water. The best part is that you can actually play with the water. Everyone in the group stayed to admired the Crown Fountain.

From there we went to Cloud Gate (I believe it is mostly known as The Bean). This is the oldest thing of Chicago that I have memory of, like if it just grew there on it's own, and is one of the first things I think of when I think of Chicago. The Bean always looks shiny, any time of year. It always keeps its image. When everyone saw The Bean we all went underneath it and gazed at it. It feels like a whole new experience going through it and looking at the shiny Bean.

We later went to the Lurie Garden. At Lurie Garden there are all of these beautiful flowers and a nice wooden path to walk on. But my favorite part is when you can dip your feet in the nice cool water. This area was a really cool place where you can just sit down, relax, and just enjoy the moment. We were there for a bit as we talked and sat down for a bit, it was really nice there.

Our next destination was the Maggie Daley Park. But in order to cross, we had to use the long shiny pedestrian bridge. Even just walking on the wooden floor feels nice, as you hear your shoes hit the wood sound relaxing and and calm. Looking at the magnificent chrome bridge makes you feel happy, like it was meant to be there. So far it's my favorite bridge and always will be.

But once we had finally crossed the bridge to get to the park we had lots of fun. It the was the most entertaining part of the day. We played in the tire swings, the big slides, and even got wet. Everyone had a really great time, the day was perfect, but it was time to go home. Not once throughout the day did I ever see someone having a bad day. All I heard were the cries of laughter and joy. And that is something marvelous about Chicago: Chicago is the place where you can just go out and have a great time.

Steven S. is a fourteen-year-old kid with lots of wins in Fortnite and in PUBG. He attends Jovita Idar Academy where he learned to play guitar (and is still learning), and outside of school he is learning the piano. Steven likes many different activities that ranges from playing outside to getting creative by crafting different props. In school, he strives to get grades higher than a C, and really tries his best. Steven also tries to be a well-trusted person with a good reputation.

MY
CIRCUMSTANCE

BY JAYLIN F.

My Chicago is only judged by the experiences I've had and my state of mind during the experiences.

My Chicago has too many factors to devote one opinion to it.

My Chicago has lives that will never move farther than its borders and souls that will never move from their resting places.

My Chicago streets have blood that stains the lives of so many. It makes me wonder how the lake stays so blue.

My Chicago is carved with history,

from my father who was left to strangers and now has carvings of his own,

to my mother whose silence also dwells within me as much as it still resides within her.

But maybe despite my view, you could judge your own experience based on how you feel about Chicago.

So maybe if I smile in return you might actually forget long enough to disregard what I say and forge your own view on this city.

Jaylin Le'Antwoine F. is seventeen years old and was born in Chicago. He moved to Carbondale, IL at the age of two with his father, mother and brother. At the age of seven, he moved back to Chicago with his sister and soon-to-be stepfather. A year later, in 2009, his sister passed. Fast forward to November 2015, he got sick and stopped going to school because of his illness for about a year. Jaylin then enrolled at Pathways in Education.

YOU HEAR THAT?

BY BRIAN F.

"You hear that?" Gio said.

"Bro, what you talking about?" I replied.

"It's footsteps, bro," Gio said.

Danny turned down the music and said, "Bro, nah man."

Then it got quiet and we listened, hearing only the steps getting closer to the room that we were in. The footsteps stopped. I thought, Time stops, every second passing slower than the other. Then a scream shocked us.

Fuck.

"Get the fuck out on your knees with your hands up!"

We opened the door, and there were two men dressed in all black with guns pointed at the door, then at us as we each got out of the small room.

"Lay on the ground!"

Lying on the cold dusty ground with my face smack center on the floor and my arms and legs spread apart, I tried to take a peek at what was happening.

"What are you doing here?"

Lying in the far back with only a glimpse of the two security guards, I peeked and saw one of them moving in on Danny to search him while the other guard covered him. As the guard patted down Danny from hands to feet, I looked over to Gio, who was trying to sneak some paint markers out from his pocket.

"Stop! Stop! Stop! What do you have?"

"I have nothing, I wasn't doing anything, man!" Gio said.

The guard then got away from Danny and jumped on Gio, lifting him up from the ground and throwing everything from his pockets onto the floor. The guard took a second look at the markers that he had taken from Gio's pockets. The guard threw Gio to the ground and put him in handcuffs.

Great, it's my turn. I honestly don't have anything to worry about, right? Oh, nah, my guy. Giant L just taken, bro lows. I hope to God I have my wallet with my ID on me.

The guard then picked me up and started digging through my pockets, finding nothing but my phone, wallet and keys. In the wallet were 50 bucks and my school ID. Patting me down and finding nothing, he put everything back in my pockets, then turned me around with my hands behind my back and threw handcuffs on me.

Aye, yo, my guy. What you doing? My dude just grabbed my dick like he's my female or some shit. Yo, wait. What you doing, my guy? Oh, hell nah, this dude gay.

The guard then walked over to his partner and pulled him to the side and talked low so that we couldn't hear, but I knew it couldn't be good.

"Is there anything in that room shouldn't be in there?"

"Oh yeah, my guy already knows just my book bag that has all my pills. Bet, I could prove that they're all mine, though," I said.

One of the guards walked over to the room where we had been and came back out with my black bag in his right hand. Moving back to his partner's side, he opened my bag in front of all of us. He took out all my papers and books and found yellow and black caution tape, three old cameras, and two cans of blue and red spray paint. It's over, I'm just done. Now everything is just--damn, I knew we should've just got out when we could. Great!

"So you're the ones that been tagging around here, huh?"

"No, sir. It wasn't us," I replied.

"Right. Let's go."

One of the guards picked up Danny and Gio and walked them out of the warehouse while the other guard watched over me until it was my turn to be taken outside. I tried raising my head off the dusty ground so my face wouldn't be covered with dirt, but it just made my neck hurt. They finally picked me up and brought me to where Danny and Gio were outside. We waited in front of the warehouse where the wind blew the coldest touch of air I had ever felt at our faces. After a few minutes, I could feel nothing but the cuffs on my hands getting sharper with every blast the wind blew at us. Wearing nothing more than a windbreaker and an old Bears hoodie to protect me from the freezing cold, I felt as if I was already freezing alive. Noticing that the two guards were talking, I tried to listen in. I couldn't hear a word of what they were saying because of the wind blowing, so I focus on trying to stay warm. I did hear one word as clear as day.

"Police."

Well, there's no point worrying about anything now. It's too cold for worrying. Jesus, guy. My only hope is to get out of here now. I don't really care what they were talking about or where they take us, just not here.

Pulling up slowly in a blue and white van were the Chicago police. They came out of the van and straight away walked over to the guards to figure out what had happened. While waiting to be questioned by the police officers, the only thought in my head was, When are they taking us away from this frozen hell? The guards already had our information, so I figured we would be out in no time. The police removed the handcuffs the guards had put on us and put their own cuffs on our wrists.

When we go to the police station, we cleaned off the dust and dirt from our clothes and waited for the police to finish our paperwork. Then they moved us to a room on a higher floor to get our fingerprints and pictures taken. After that, they placed us in a holding room, where we waited to be picked up by our families. While waiting in that room, I could only think about how simple today's plan was. Take some pictures and chill out with the boys. Not really too much of a plan to fuck up, but that's not how it went down. How do I even show my face to my family? What do I even say to them? Geez, it's only getting worse thinking about this, but not thinking is what got me in here.

"This guy!" I said.

"What?" Danny replied.

"This some bullshit!" I exclaimed.

"Bro, I know," Gio replied.

"Y'all gonna be good after this shit?" I asked.

"I don't even know, bro," Gio replied.

"Pff, nothing to do about it now," I added.

As I was sitting back and trying to clear my head, the door opened with the officer calling my name. I was the first to get out of the police station. Shaking up with Danny and Gio, I walked down to the front desk, where I saw my mother's disappointed face. I knew I'd been bombing life, but when I saw that much hurt in her eyes, it hurt more than anything I had ever felt before in my life. An officer walked up from behind me with my black bag and the stuff I had taken from the warehouse. My mother had signed me out, and we wasted no time getting to the car to leave this place. We rode in the car in complete silence until my mother started to speak with a tone I had never heard her use with me. It was as if I had backstabbed her, someone who had always been there for me, and was hearing her final thoughts.

"Why do you continue to put yourself down? Don't you think about how hard I work to get to where we are? Your father doesn't help, nor do you or your sister. How long do you think I'm going to be around? How long do you think life is going to be this easy? You're the one with the opportunity to help us. Are you really going to waste it doing nothing? That's not the man I raised you to become. If you choose to continue with this shit, you can get the fuck out."

Every word that came out of her mouth got stuck in my head and hit me deep down in my heart. I knew full well that playing these games was not going to get me anywhere. Thinking about the choices I made only showed me that I had nothing to show. I was just a boy trying to live the wrong life, throwing away everything that would help me. Looking back, I started to see how so many of my choices and decisions had led me to that moment. With how thoughtless I had been with my decisions, a negative outcome was practically inevitable. Learning from this outcome sparked a change in my mind: I didn't want to live without a purpose, and I didn't to be forced to live a meaningless life doing something I didn't want to do because of the decisions I had made in my youth.

It's been two years now since this happened to me, and I've mostly forgotten about it, but what I have kept is everything I learned during that time of being lost. I spent a lot of time trying to find an answer to the question, "What's going to be my purpose?" I realized the truth: Life is hard, but I'm not only living for myself, but for everyone in my life. Even if things start to get worse, I can't run away or give up because there are people counting on me. My nephew, who is basically like a little brother to me, is eventually going to face similar enemies that he's going to have to overcome. I had no one to guide me, but he will have me there to guide him. I'm here to share what I've learned and to watch out for him. I want him to think of me when he needs that support or motivation.

Brian F. is eighteen years old and was born and raised in Chicago. He grew up on the North Side and moved to the South Side when he was thirteen. He's a man of different arts and has talents in a variety of fine arts, including photography, visual art, speaking/acting, and dancing. Family is the biggest thing to him. He strives to succeed and hopes to keep moving forward and helping the people around him.

THE MUSEUMS
OF CHICAGO

BY MANUEL C.

Chicago is a fun place to be,
Lots of places to go and things to see.

Especially the museums, oh what a sight,
Once you're in them, you're as free as a kite.

Flying around towards all the exhibits,
While learning some tidbits.

All of the knowledge entering your brain,
And you feel as sweet as a candy cane.

All the colors swirling together,
It'll stick with you forever.

All the cool artifacts,
Shown to you like shiny nick-nacks.

Shining as bright as gold
It's hard to believe some of them are hundreds of years old.

All the friendly people giving us tours,
Almost like we were drawn in by lures.

The Aquarium especially, when you see the fishes swimming to their lair,
You can't help but to just sit and stare.

When the fishes swim in their school,
I think it's really cool.

And in the Field Museum when you see the dinosaur bones,
You just stop like cars at traffic cones.

As you stand there in awe,
You think something this amazing should be against the law.

When you're at the Museum of Science and Industry there is no end to fun,
From the moment you enter until you leave your smile is as bright as the sun.

This is one of the many things that makes Chicago special to me,
Oh what a wonderful place to be.

Manuel C. is thirteen years old. He goes to school at Jovita Idar and has been living in Chicago ever since he was born. In summer, he likes to play baseball, basketball and soccer. He also likes rock/alternative rock, metal and early 2000's music. He dislikes when people refer to his music as "emo music." He also dislikes when people don't have their facts right, like saying they like a certain album from his favorite band but then they say their favorite song from that album it is not at all from that album. He is also TERRIFIED!!!! of spiders and heights. When he grows up he wants to be a chemical engineer, a video game designer, or start a really great band.

LOVE
IN CHICAGO

BY JUST

I found love in Chicago right next door from my current home, right off the infamous 79th street, here I witnessed friends fall to stray bullets, where the only focus is you thinking how you gon' get paid or if you going to survive until the next day.

Growing up in Chicago, it it was harder living in a poverty struck community, where shootings happen everyday. As I grew up my family struggled, so having money was my main goal. But I never thought I would put so much focus in a female. Growing up I had a friend next door whose aunt was same age as me. I kinda had crush on since I was a kid and I knew her for years. I always tried to get her attention and be on a higher level from being just friends, despite the fact that wanting to be with her was blocking my focus from priorities. I didn't care. It took me two years to actually make her mine, but it was worth it. She wasn't technically from Chicago, so you might say that she was different from the other females. Despite the life I led, she wanted me to do better in Chicago. In Chicago, it's hard. Trying not to become a product of your environment is hard in my neighborhood. I started falling off from school by doing more activity in the streets and making bad decisions.

Most females that are normally from Chicago entertain and support that behavior because of the hype and that's what they search for in most guys.

In Chicago, inner city neighborhoods such as Auburn, Gresham, Englewood, etc. young men like myself are more focused on making money to provide for ourselves or our families and trying to live life bout having to worry about someone taking our lives. We rarely be about love. We really just see most of these females as pleasure nothing serious. But like I said, "the girl I knew was different." ut my years I chased her to be by her side. I grew up anted to be different. When we finally got together, ct of my life to where I came from, to the fact I streets and stop getting arrested, and a whole though she made me want to stop them things, ome a disappointment to her.

I started cheating on her. Being young as I am, I never expected to fall in love with her. I started off with a mindset that was strictly about making money and staying away from love, but at the moment I wasn't making the money. I was still struggling right along with my family I was trying to provide for.

And to make things worse I was going through my own personal problems, trying to deal with gang related deaths of the friends I lost and problems I had at school and at home and nobody would listen besides one person and that was girl I was madly in love with. She always listened, always was there when I needed her, and always tried to steer me in the right direction. I came to my final decision and knew I wanted to be with her but two years later after being together, cheating and not listening to her, left me at the end not having nobody because we ended up breaking up. That was the very first love I found in Chicago. I had someone that bettered my situation in every way but being dumb and hardheaded left me without her.

Justin R. is seventeen years old and was born and raised in Chicago. He enjoys making music with his friends with intentions of one day making it to the industry, but at the moment he's more focused on finishing school and working.

MY COMMUNITY

BY ANNA E.

In Austin, all we see is abandoned buildings, children getting beat tryna be like their dads that's keepin' that heat, mothers can't get on their feet so they were told to take a seat but at grandma's house everyone feels safe because there's no other place where kids can't reach the mace but I mean it's not a race they just need some space 'cause otherwise they'll catch a case with a 'lil puppy face they say they have an ace but they're not going to be there during the chase…Can you blame 'em doe that's all they know they used to fighting for everything even if it's just to go out and play in the snow well damn how do they know if it's their time to go they used to their mom being shouted down and called a hoe but that's Austin -- there's no unity, barely a community.

Anna E. is a ninth grader at Michele Clark High School. Her favorite ice cream is strawberry shortcake. She likes to run track and play basketball and volleyball. She loves to sleep, eat, and laugh. She is from the West Side of Chicago. Her favorite restaurant is Als Under the L. She loves their steak burgers. Her favorite song is "Ice Melts" by Drake. She has eight other siblings and one single parent. She is the third youngest. She has very long, curly, pretty hair. She is like Helen Keller to the B.S., she can't see it or hear it. She is very calm until she gets around certain people then she acts very outrageous and rowdy. When she gets older, she will own her own business so no one will be able to tell her how to run her business.

TRES TACOS DE ASADA

BY EDGAR S.

I open the door of the main entrance
Coming home from a long day at school.
I can hear my mom in the kitchen cooking food.
I ask how her day went and help her with stuff.

Hiss, sizzle, pop.
The smell of the carne asada
Hits me in the face
Chop, chop, chop, chop, chop, chop, chop
Cebolla y cilantro meet their end.
The spicy aroma joins the scent of frying meat.

Sizzle, sizzle, sizzle, sizzle, sizzle, plop
The tortillas are moving back and forth
From the plates and the pans
You can feel how soft the tortillas are when they're ready.

Ding, ding, ding, ding, ding
Dad, mom, and brother at the table,
The glass cups are being poured with agua de horchata
We're ready to eat these delicious tacos de carne asada.

When were done eating we get up and put our plates
In the sink and we say thank you for the food she made
For us. This is my Chicago: coming home from school and
Eating delicious.

Edgar S. is fourteen years old and goes to Jovita Idar Academy. He lives in Chicago. His favorite sport is soccer and when he grows up, he wants to be a professional soccer player. Edgar lives with his mom, dad, brother, and sister. He also has a dog named Marley.

THE MILLENIUM MEMORY

BY NICHOLA H.

Chicago, to me, is everything. It's my hometown, it's where I have spent all of my lifetime. Even half of my dad's family lives here. It's where I have my family and friends. But this specific memory is what makes this my own memoir.

This memory all took place with a special person that, to this day, I kinda recognize her as my third "grandma". This special person was a person that has known both my parents ever since they got here to the U.S. I call her "grandma" because she took care of me when both my parents worked and I had to no one to take care of me. She was very short, she was kinda old, and she was ready for that age.

I was six years old and I still haven't forgotten this at all. My grandma decided to take both me and brother downtown so we wouldn't be bored at the house that day. And, wow, I don't think that I even knew what downtown even was back then, to be honest. Which I don't think we were supposed to, but oh well.

That day it was a really nice and sunny day with at least 75 degrees on that scale. We took the orange line all the way to the center of Chicago, known as downtown, but, wow, was it beautiful. The big tall skyscrapers in the blue sky that looked like it stretched for miles and miles. I'm not gonna leave this part but I was really, really scared to look up at the sky, because when you would look up all you would see were all these huge skyscrapers. I was really terrified because I thought that eventually they were gonna fall on me and crush me. And the lake was like almost as clear as a shiny diamond, though we didn't go in it.

We went to Millennium Park to walk around and I actually was really shocked at watching all these people walk around this park that day. There was this really huge guy walking around on two sticks literally on his feet! He shook our hands and literally had to bend over to shake our hands, he was about twenty inches taller than me. I even have the picture where I'm meeting and shaking this giant dude's hand.

That day I had so much fun walking around downtown, Millennium Park and all spending the day with that special person. That whole day is what made me write about my Chicago which is what this memoir was all about.

Nichola H. is a fourteen year old at ACERO Jovita Idar Elementary School. He is the oldest and has three younger siblings. He is trying his hardest to become a great role model for all his siblings. His major goals in life are to become a mechanical engineer and to stick to a sport that is gonna keep him active while alive and to have a family. He's planning to finish school and to graduate so that he actually accomplishes his life goals. He loves to goof off a lot, maybe a little too much but oh well.

MY LIFE

BY JEREMY R.

This mask on my face is all you see,

This is the pain you'll never see.

This smile shows happiness but that's just ignorance to the sadness deep in me,

I remember back in the trailer in Seeman Homes,

Comin' from a broken home with no father, left alone.

Drunk stepdad was quite violent,

But Mamma showed how quickly she could dethrone.

She disowned,

Threw him on the streets to be alone.

But Mamma never let him go,

Always said he would never change,

Just always left in disarray,

Still remember the day when Dan broke her face,

That's a disgrace.

Knife to my throat I was ready to end all,

Never could do it, couldn't leave my brothers in this suffering world of pain,

Had no food but a leftover candy cane,

Knew it was foolish,

Looked at my mom and knew we could do this,

Told myself it would be okay.

Then Mamma started getting into pills,

Always knew that shit killed.

She lay in bed all day, like Mamma this isn't you,

But she never knew,

How I saw it all.

No one knows how I feel when I fall.

Oxycontin devouring her self conscious,
But she didn't see how she was being cruel.
Most days only got food from school,
Like Ma, we need you,
We need you to get up, we got no food,
Started hustlin' the neighbors so the fridge wasn't a useless tool,
We used to eat out the garbage
Like a racoon.

Then a time in my life came were I could pick and choose,
To be with my father after many years,
Now I look him in the eyes without a thought in my mind,
Now I thank my mom for my life cause she tried,
But sometimes it's hard lookin' through these eyes,
And all the times I cried and my mom knew why.

Jeremy R. is a raconteur from Chicago who moved around a lot, from Chicago to Indiana all the way to Ohio, and finally back to Chicago. He was raised ghetto and struggled as a kid. He has seen the bad and the good, and after going to Pathways, he found a new hope in people once again.

MY CHICAGO

BY ASHLEY O.

Walk down the crowded streets of downtown Chicago
Look high at the tall buildings that ever so lightly kiss the clouds
See below at the river that runs through the entire city
Smell the delicacies that our city is known for
Pizza, hot dogs, and more.
Let the city wind blow through your hair
And listen as the cars race down Lower Wacker
My city is beautiful and I want to share it with everyone!
No one is more proud than a Chicagoan
And no other city is as wonderful as my Chicago.

Ashley O. is nineteen years old. Born and raised in Chicago's Little Village neighborhood, she moved to the Chicago Lawn neighborhood when she was thirteen. She loves to read and listen to music during her free time. Her favorite sport is baseball, and she loves the White Sox. She enjoys Chicago's warm sunny days and even the cold winter nights. She is excited to go to college after graduating and finding a career that she enjoys. She looks up to her mother for being so hardworking and loving and her grandfather, who was respected and loved by everyone and was also her father figure for most of her teenage years. She hopes to one day make them proud.

SUMMER
IN CHICAGO

BY CHRISTIAN M.

I wake up inside my beautiful city known as Chicago. I awake with laziness still in my eyes, thinking to myself that I still want to go back to sleep. But today I am going to the park. Where I hear all children laughing 'cause it's summer and all the kids are having fun and the weather is so nice out and the sun is bright.

I walk with my cousins with round and colorful soccer balls in their hands just ready to go all out on that field, but as soon as I get there, there is still that squeaky swing I've been seeing ever since I was little. It's my favorite spot to go every time I go to the park. When you are on that rusted old swing you feel the wind going in your face as you go higher and higher and feel that cold air.

But there's still more things to do in this park. I've been going since I was a toddler. There is also every kid's favorite thing to do in park: whirl slides kids go on for the thrill. I don't know if I have to explain how it feels to be on a slide.

There are so many play things to do in this park. What me and my cousins sometimes do is play soccer and every time I play it I have the feeling of nervousness always. When you try to take the ball away a drop of sweat slides down from my forehead to my nose and I finally get the ball. I am rushing to the goal, feeling the wind behind me I get pass both defenders. And I shoot...everything goes in slow motion as the ball hits the net with a swoosh and I hear my cousin shout that our team is victorious.

When we start to leave the sun is going down. Every single one of us is tired and we hear cars passing by and hear the stomp of people's feet. When I get home, I plop down on my bed, tired, thinking in my head about what this city Chicago has for me tomorrow.

Christian M. is fourteen years old and has been living in Chicago ever since he could walk. He likes to mess around a lot and play some video games and also have fun.

GROWING
UP CHICAGO

BY SAMANTHA B.

I will live at 950 N. Michigan Avenue,
In a one bedroom apartment on the top floor.
My apartment will have the grandest view of them all;
Letting in the bright lights and hum of the city that will invade the space.
I will be able to see Navy Pier's night time fireworks,
Maggie Daley's lively scene
And the vivid shine of the Sears tower.

The rooms in my apartment will reflect every part of my personality-
From the Selena posters flooding the walls along with pictures
From my "Growing Up Mariachi" childhood.
Frames of my friends and I in our suits,
Playing at the Copernicus Center, splashing in the pool in Arizona
And smiling in front of the Bean.

My favorite classical music record, Kreisler's Gypsy Caprice will be playing in the background.
It will echo off the walls and resonate with the warm sunlight that enters through the window.

I will be a Psychiatrist working Downtown and wearing all of the big brands that I dreamed of as a child.
I will finally be able to afford the Gucci bags and Christian Louboutin shoes I've always wanted.

I know that it won't be easy to get there.
I know that I will have to work very hard to fulfill my dream,
But that won't stop me.
Chicago has provided me with a goal
And I'm going to make it a reality.

Samantha B. is an eighth grader at Jovita Idar, living on the southside of Chicago with her family and three cats. Samantha plays the violin and has been doing so for four years. She plays in a youth Mariachi group which has provided her with many opportunities to travel the country and play music alongside her friends; so far, her favorite trip has been to Arizona. She hopes to study Psychology while continuing her music career, but first she hopes to attend Whitney Young Magnet High School–one of Chicago's most prestigious schools. Her music idol is the late Selena Quintanilla.

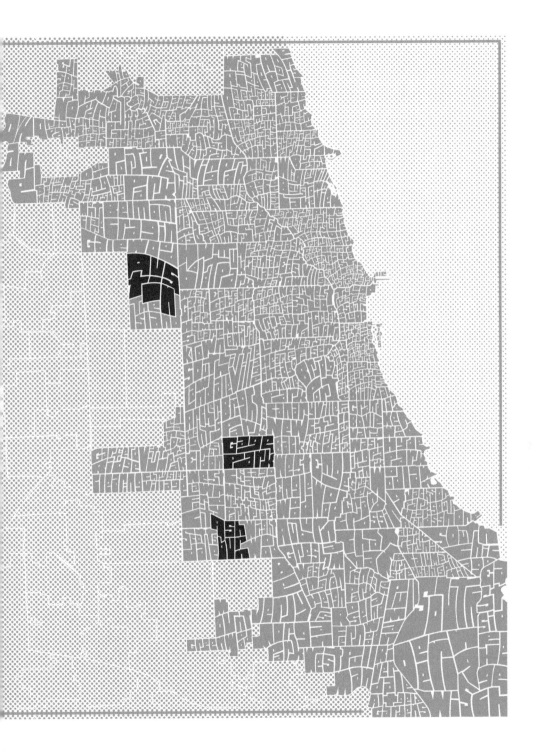

AFTERWORD

BY MEG MORRISON

In the beginning, it was chaos. When we first began discussing the possibility of publishing their writing in this book, students' reactions were very mixed. Some faces glowed with enthusiasm, but others clouded over in worry.

"Do we have to?" they asked. They worried that their stories were too personal to share, that they would censor themselves if they knew they were writing for an audience. I reassured them that no, they didn't have to publish if they didn't want to, but they had to submit their pieces at the end of the semester as their final project. Relieved, they started brainstorming and bouncing ideas off me and their peers.

The first drafts were the most difficult. Some stories flowed immediately, and others took a little more prompting, nudging, and cajoling to get them onto the page. Once their first drafts were done and it was time to revise, they started to realize the reality of publication. There was pressure, but there was also possibility. With each stroke of a pen and clack of a keyboard, they were opening windows onto worlds their readers might never have seen before.

They began to consider what their writing might mean to Chicago, to the world. They wondered whether their words would change minds, would change lives. Writing lit a flame within them, giving them a chance to illuminate a piece of their world for the rest of us or disperse the darkness they had been carrying within them. They realized the potential power of their words.

My colleagues and I saw it in the shy smiles tugging at the corners of our students' mouths when we conferenced with them to discuss their latest revisions and revelations. We heard it in the feverish clicking and clacking of the keyboard keys as they poured their stories onto the page, in the glimmer of pride in their voices when they told their peers what they were working on. We felt it in the rejoicing when a piece was finally finished, polished for publication.

These writers showed us so many sides of the city they call home. Reading their stories is like twirling a kaleidoscope, each rotation reflecting a different view of the beauty and the pain, the simple and the extraordinary that fill these pages. Their words reverberate with us like the deep rumbling of the L, pushing us to consider this city from their point of view.

As I write this, I can only imagine how these writers will react when they pick this book up for the first time. How their hands will reach out eagerly, ready to feel the weight of their accomplishments in their palms. How their fingers will flip frantically through the pages while their eyes scan for their names. How their voices will fill the air with exclamations of joy when they find what they're looking for.

How their words will change this city.

Meg Morrison is a high school English teacher who is incredibly thankful that she gets to spend her days reading, writing, and discussing literature and life with truly inspirational young people. Pretty much everyone who knows Meg is aware of her deep and abiding love for the Harry Potter series. She strives to make her classroom as welcoming and nurturing for her students as Hogwarts is for Harry. She spends her free time reading novels, baking sweet treats, and traveling the world.

About the Young Authors Book Project

Every year, 826CHI develops a special in-school partnership with one or more teachers and their classrooms to collaborate on a Young Authors Book Project (YABP). Led by experienced staff with the support of 826CHI's trained volunteer cohort, this year-long project engages students in the experience of writing, editing, and designing a professional publication of their work. At the end of the project, students will celebrate the release of their book alongside Chicago's vibrant literary community at the Printers Row Lit Fest. And as of last year, the Chicago Public Library began carrying 826CHI's student publications in all 77 of its branches, which means that YABP student authors will be able to find their own published stories in neighborhoods across the city.

About the 2017-18 Project

This year, 826CHI partnered with the 8th-12th grades at Jovita Idar Elementary School (Gage Park), Michele Clark High School (Austin) and Pathways in Education (Ashburn) to counter the negative narrative that is often imposed upon Chicago by the media and by non-Chicago residents. This YABP expresses the inner beauty of Chicago through the experiences and writing of our students. 826CHI is not denying that there is violence in Chicago, and that it affects the lives of our students, but the story is not complete if it just stops there.

Students began the project with a field trip to the 826CHI writing lab. During the field trip they (re)discovered Chicago via its art, musicians, authors, and neighborhoods to begin formulating their own Chicago story through a series of generative writing activities. After the field trip, students were tasked with writing a piece in the form of essay, memoir, or poem that represents the beauty of their Chicago.

In this book readers have the opportunity to meditate on Chicago through beautiful crafted pieces of writing by young people from all over the city. We hope readers will be inspired to write about their Chicago so included in the book are the writing prompts students used as springboards for their own reflection and writing. These prompts can be used for aspiring writers of any age and in any capacity from journal writing to in-classroom work.

Through the writing and stories of the young people that live here our hope is to broaden the perception of Chicago and its people. We hope readers connect with the stories by the young people in this book and begin to take that connection off the page to cultivate a new relationship with Chicago and its people.

For more information or to learn how to bring a project like this to your classroom or community, contact 826CHI's Director of Programs, Maria Villarreal, Maria@826chi.org.

Teacher Bios:

Michele Clark Magnet High School

Ms. Hughes (grade 24) loves the Harry Potter series and hip hop. She is originally from Davenport, Iowa so sweet corn is obviously one of her favorite foods. She has been teaching for eighteen years and surprisingly to her, has developed a love for teaching poetry and coaching her students in the world's largest youth poetry festival, Louder than a Bomb, for which she was named the 2010 "Coach of the Year." Chance the Rapper is her favorite artist and she has a picture of him hugging her which she thinks is awesome.

Pathways in Education—Ashburn

Megan Kehoe is an English teacher, hustler, and cheeseburger enthusiast, who likes chill vibes and staying hydrated. When Megan is not teaching she is probably laughing at vanity license plates and children on leashes. She is currently working on her Master's degree in Literacy at DePaul University.

Maria Rivera is not a professional wrestler. She is an educator, storyteller, and writer. Originally from Detroit, Chicago is her second home. It has brought her great pain, and exponential love. Maria feels the most in love with Chicago when she is collaborating with it's educators, artists, and storytellers to amplify young people's voices. Pathways in Education, is her current teaching home.

Jovita Idar Academy

Ms. Horwitz, soon to be Mrs. Bjornrud, has been herding cats - apologies, she meant teaching eighth grade - for six years. She absolutely loves working with this age group. Working with eighth grade helps remind her to look at the humorous side of life, and that its ok to laugh at a lame joke every now and then. She moved to Chicago in 2012 with her two dogs and fell in love with the city. Her favorite aspect of Chicago? The amazing street art that brightens almost every corner; each one represents the vast diversity of Chicago that makes this city such a special place to live.

Acknowledgments:

We are incredibly grateful for the generosity of our donors, who fund our programs and publications. Thank you for giving our students the opportunity to become published authors and share their stories with the world. You help them creatively engage with their community, enriching the lives of their families, teachers, and peers throughout our city. This publication was made possible in part by the Colonel Stanley R. McNeil Foundation, Bank of America, N.A., Trustee; The Donley Foundation; The Judy Family Foundation; Justine Jentes and Dan Kuruna; Jan and Sarah Zasowki; Brenda and Girish Gehani; and Christine and Thomas Quinn. Thank you, Diane Quinn, for your tremendous generosity in supporting our mission.

This project would not have been possible without the hard work of the students, teachers, and administrators at Pathways in Education, Michele Clark High School, and Jovita Idar Academy. Meg Morrison, Megan Kehoe, Maria Rivera, Melissa Hughes, and Michelle Horwitz, your tireless dedication to your students is an absolute inspiration. We'd like to give a hearty round of applause to the brave students who shared their lives with us and from whom we can learn so much. Extra claps for the student ambassadors who contributed to the student foreword: Jaylin, Paola, Jamia, Izzy, Jonathan, Hannah, and Riley.

Thank you so incredibly much to Joe Mills, an incredible artist who used his considerable talents to illuminate our students' work. Eve L. Ewing managed to step away from her crowded schedule to write a phenomenal foreword that highlights and champions the work in this book. Thank you, Eve, for appreciating our students as much as we do!

Our warmest thanks to Molly Sprayregen, Shannon Barry, and Kate Kowalski who gave their time to aid students with the writing process. Shannon and Kate also went above and beyond in developing this manuscript, from first field trip to last edit. Thank you to the cohort of copy editors for this book: Shannon, Kate, Breanne Johnson, and Mary Norkol, who ensured that each students' voice got the right amount of polish to truly shine through.

The intern cohort of 2017-2018 are astoundingly talented, intelligent, big-hearted, and hard-working. This project would not have existed without their commitment and skill. Thank you, thank you, thank you to Shannon Barry, Alex Boone, Megan Cho, Connie Chu, Taylor Fustin, Amina Hodzic, Breanne Johnson, Kate Kowalski, Emma Kupor, Mackenzie Lynch, Mussad Muhammad, Mary Norkol, Talia Prusky, Qiaira Riley, Mercury Rivera, Jazmine Rodriguez, and Mahalia Sobhani.

Finally, thank you, reader, for picking up this book of student writing. The further voices from Chicago are amplified, the quicker we can add to the one-sided view people have of this city. Please share these memoirs and poems with people in and out of Chicago so they can have the opportunity to experience some of what this city has to offer.

About 826CHI:

826CHI ("eight-two-six Chicago") is a nonprofit organization dedicated to supporting students ages six to 18 with their creative and expository writing skills, and to helping teachers inspire their students to write. Our services are structured around the understanding that great leaps in learning can happen with individualized attention, and that strong writing skills are fundamental to future success.

With this in mind, we provide after-school tutoring, creative writing workshops, in-school residencies, field trips, support for English Language Learners, and publishing opportunities for Chicago youth—all at absolutely no cost to Chicago's schools, teachers, and students.

We strive for all of our programs to strengthen each student's power to express ideas effectively, creatively, confidently, and in their individual voice by providing them a safe space to be their most creative selves.

Learn more at: www.826chi.org.

OUR PROGRAMS

826CHI's free programs reach students at every opportunity—in school, after school, in the evenings, and on the weekends.

After-School Tutoring and Writing

826CHI is packed four afternoons a week with students in first through eighth grade working on their homework and sharpening their creative writing skills. Volunteer tutors help students with any and all homework assignments and lead students in daily creative and expository writing activities. Student writing created during tutoring is published in chapbooks throughout the year, and we frequently host student readings for parents, tutors, families, and the greater 826CHI community.

Field Trips

On weekday mornings throughout the school year, we host classes from Chicago schools for lively, writing-based Field Trips at our writing center. Teachers may choose from a wide range of programs, such as our Storytelling & Bookmaking Field Trip, which focuses on plot and character development, or "I Remember . . ." Memoir Writing, in which teenage students transform powerful memories into reflective prose.

In-School Partnerships

Because it can be difficult for teachers and students to make it to our center during the school day, 826CHI brings itself into schools across the city. Thanks to our dedicated volunteer pool, we're able to bring a team writing coaches to give individualized attention to students as they tackle various projects. Do you have an idea for a writing project and could use the assistance of 826CHI's educators and volunteers?

Workshops

Designed to foster creativity, strengthen writing skills, and provide students with a forum to execute projects they otherwise might not have the support to undertake, 826CHI Workshops are led by talented volunteers—including published authors, educators, playwrights, chefs, and other artists—on Saturdays and throughout the summer.

Teen Writers Studio

826CHI's Teen Writers Studio (or "TWS") is a year-long creative writing workshop that connects high school students to fellow writers, including peers and older professionals in the field. It's open to anyone in 9th-12th grade and welcomes youth from all over the city. TWS members meet twice each month to write together, talk about writing, and produce a literary chapbook each June. If you're into any of the above, this space is for you.

Publishing

At 826CHI, each student is challenged to produce their finest writing, knowing that their words will have the opportunity to be read, laughed at, wept over, or deeply pondered by their family, friends, and folks they may not even know. By the power of a very heavy binding machine, we are able to assemble many of the students' pieces into handsome books in-house. When not laying out, cutting up, and binding at 826CHI, we send special collections of writing (like this one!) to a professional printer with gigantic machines in order to put together a well-bound publication.

The Young Authors Book Project

We're proud of everything we publish at 826CHI, but we get particularly excited about our annual Young Author's Book Project ("YABP"), in which we partner with a local school to produce an anthology of student work. Over the course of a full school year, our writing coaches work individually with students to help them clarify their voices and polish their drafts. A self-selected group of students and volunteers form an Ambassador Cohort to co-write an introduction, and each YABP is also introduced with a foreword by a professional author. Every June, we release this publication to raucous applause at the historic Printers Row Lit Fest, where students are invited to read their work to an audience full of their peers, family members, 826CHI supporters, and strangers. These books are sold at bookstores big and small all over the country and are a huge source of pride for 826CHI and our authors. Flip to page 305 to read about our other Young Authors Book Projects.

The Wicker Park Secret Agent Supply Co.

826CHI shares its space with the Wicker Park Secret Agent Supply Co., a store with a not-so-secret mission. Our unique products encourage creative writing and imaginative play, and trigger new adventures for agents of all ages. Every purchase supports 826CHI's free programming, so visit us at 1276 N Milwaukee Ave in Wicker Park to pick up writing tools, fancy notebooks, assorted fake moustaches and other stellar disguises, books from local publishers, our latest student publications, and much more!

Or, visit us online at www.secretagentsupply.com.

Staff

Kendra Curry-Khanna, Executive Director
Julia Clausen, Data & Impact Associate (AmeriCorps VISTA)
Ola Faleti, Development Coordinator
Gaby FeBland, Communications Coordinator
Gerardo Galan, Program Coordinator
Waringa Hunja, Publications Coordinator
Melissa Kirk, Volunteer Coordinator (AmeriCorps VISTA)
Mackenzie Lynch, Commuications Associate (AmeriCorps VISTA)
David Pintor, Volunteer Manager
Molly Sprayregen, Program Coordinator
Tyler Stoltenberg, Operations Manager
Molly Fannin, Director of Development
Maria Villarreal, Director of Programs

2017-2018 Interns

Shannon Barry
Alex Boone
Megan Cho
Connie Chu
Taylor Fustin
Amina Hodzic
Breanne Johnson
Kate Kowalski
Emma Kupor

Mackenzie Lynch
Mussad Muhammad
Mary Norkol
Talia Prusky
Qiaira Riley
Mercury Rivera
Jazmine Rodriguez
Mahalia Sobhani

Board of Directors

Sameer Gadkaree, Chair
Kathleen St. Louis Caliento, Vice-Chair
Josh Gantz, Treasurer
Alexia Elejalde-Ruiz, Secretary
Kevin Boehm
Brenda Flores Gehani

Ryan Hubbard
Tony Malcoun
Christine Quinn
Kashif Shaikh
Hilary Ward